AF700677

Medical Law in France

Medical Law in France

Second Edition

Anne-Marie Duguet

This book was originally published as a monograph in the International Encyclopaedia of Laws/Medical Law.

Founding Editor: Roger Blanpain
General Editor: Frank Hendrickx
Volume Editor: Herman Nys

Wolters Kluwer

Published by:
Kluwer Law International B.V.
PO Box 316
2400 AH Alphen aan den Rijn
The Netherlands
E-mail: international-sales@wolterskluwer.com
Website: lrus.wolterskluwer.com

Sold and distributed in North, Central and South America by:
Wolters Kluwer Legal & Regulatory U.S.
7201 McKinney Circle
Frederick, MD 21704
United States of America
Email: customer.service@wolterskluwer.com

Sold and distributed in all other countries by:
Air Business Subscriptions
Rockwood House
Haywards Heath
West Sussex
RH16 3DH
United Kingdom
Email: international-customerservice@wolterskluwer.com

DISCLAIMER: The material in this volume is in the nature of general comment only. It is not offered as advice on any particular matter and should not be taken as such. The editor and the contributing authors expressly disclaim all liability to any person with regard to anything done or omitted to be done, and with respect to the consequences of anything done or omitted to be done wholly or partly in reliance upon the whole or any part of the contents of this volume. No reader should act or refrain from acting on the basis of any matter contained in this volume without first obtaining professional advice regarding the particular facts and circumstances at issue. Any and all opinions expressed herein are those of the particular author and are not necessarily those of the editor or publisher of this volume.

Printed on acid-free paper

ISBN 978-94-035-0033-1

e-Book: ISBN 978-94-035-0034-8
web-PDF: ISBN 978-94-035-0035-5

© 2018, Kluwer Law International BV, The Netherlands

All rights reserved. No part of this publication may be reproduced, stored in a retrieval system, or transmitted in any form or by any means, electronic, mechanical, photocopying, recording, or otherwise, without the prior written permission of the publisher.

Permission to use this content must be obtained from the copyright owner. More information can be found at: lrus.wolterskluwer.com/policies/permissions-reprints-and-licensing

Printed in the United Kingdom.

The Author

Anne-Marie Duguet is MD and PhD in law, Emeritus Senior Lecturer at the Medicine Faculty Toulouse Purpan (Paul Sabatier University, France) where she teaches medical law and bioethics. She conducts her researches in the UMR INSERM Unit 1027 *Epidemiology and Public health analysis. Risks, chronic diseases and handicap.* Her research is focused on French and European Health Law, Bioethics, ethics in research, ethics in new technologies and ethics in genetics. Since 1996, she is a member of the committee for the protection of persons (CPP) (ethics committee for research) and has been the chairperson of the committee for twelve years. In the International Institute on Research in Bioethics (IIREB www.iireb.org) a network created in collaboration with Canada, she coordinates the area 'research Ethics'. As President of the ARFDM (Association for research and training on medical law www.arfdm.asso.fr), she set up an international network of young researchers in medical law and bioethics and organizes since 2006 a European summer school in bioethics and medical law in Paul Sabatier University. She has coordinated research projects supported by the Ministry of Health and has participated to several European projects. She published more than 180 scientific articles and published or contributed to twenty-five books. In 2006, she was the President of the sixteenth World Congress on Medical law in Toulouse. She is Governor of the World Association for Medical Law, member of the Advisory Board of the European Journal of Health Law, and past secretary of the European Association of Health law. She has been involved in research programmes in cooperation with Shandong University Law School, South Medical University and Kunming First Affiliated Hospital. In 2011, she has been honoured by the French decoration of 'the Palmes Académiques'.

Anne-Marie Duguet thanks Bénédicte Boyer-Bevière Assistant Professor in Private Law at University Paris 8 and Allane Madanamoothoo, Assistant Professor in Private Law at Groupe ESC Troyes for their contribution to the monograph by writing the chapter on source of medical law.

The Author

Table of Contents

Table of Contents

List of Abbreviations

ABM	Agence de la BioMédecine (Biomedicine Agency)
AFSSAPS	Agence Française de Sécurité Sanitaire des Produits de Santé (Agency for Safety of Health Products) Until 1 May 2012, replaced by ANSM
AMP/ MAP	Assistance Médicale à la Procréation (Medically Assisted Procreation)
ANESM	Agence Nationale d'Evaluation des Services Médicaux (National Agency for Evaluation of Medical Care Services)
ANSM	Agence Nationale de Sécurité du Médicament et des produits de santé (National Agency for Security of Medicines and Health Products)
ANSES	Agence Nationale de Sécurité de l'Alimentation, de l'environnement et du travail (National Agency for the Safety of Food, Environment and Labour)
ARH	Agence Regionale de l'Hospitalisation (Regional Agency for Hospitalization)
ART	Assisted Reproduction Techniques
ARS	Agence Régionale de Santé (Regional Agency for Health)
CA	Conseil d'Administration (Board of Governors)
Cass Crim	Chambre Criminelle de la Cour de cassation (Criminal Chamber of the Cassation Court)
CCI	Commission de conciliation et d'indemnisation (Commission for Conciliation and Compensation) replaces the CRCI since 2009
CCNE	Comité Consultatif National d'Ethique (National Consultative Advisory Committee on Ethics)
CEE/EEC	Communauté Economique Européenne European Economic Community
CME	Commission Médicale d'Etablissement (Medical Committee)
CMU	Couverture Maladie Universelle (Universal Health Insurance Coverage)
CNAF	Caisse Nationale des Allocations familiales (National Fund for Family Allowance)

CNAMTS	Caisse Nationale de l'Assurance Maladie des Travailleurs Salariés (National Insurance Fund for Salaried Employees)
CNAVTS	Caisse Nationale d'Assurance Vieillesse des Travailleurs Salariés (National Old-Age Insurance Fund)
CNIL	Commission Nationale Informatique et Libertés (National Commission for Data Protection and Freedoms)
CO	Conseil d'Orientation. (Orientation Council)
CRCI	Commission Régionale de Conciliation de d'Indemnisation. (Regional Commission for Mediation and Compensation)Until 2009
CS	Conseil de Surveillance (Supervisory Board)
CSP	Code de la Santé Publique (Public Health Code)
CSS	Code la Sécurité Sociale (Social Security Code)
CSSR	Centres de Soins de Suite et de Réadaptation (Centres for Care and Rehabilitation)
DDAS	Direction Départmentales des Affaires Sanitaires et Sociales (Departmental Directorate of Health and Social Affairs)
DGAS	Direction Générale de l'Action Sociale (General Directory for Social Action)
DGOS	Direction Générale de l'Organisation des Soins (General Directory for Provision of Care)
DGS	Direction Générale de la Santé (General Directory of Health)
DRASS	Direction Régionale des Affaires Sanitaires et Sociales (Regional Directory of Health and Social Affairs)
ECHR	European Convention of Human Rights
EFS	Etablissement Français du sang (French Blood Establishment)
EEG	Electroencephalogramme (Electroencephalogram)
EEZ	Exclusive Economic Zone
EPRUS	Etablissement de Prévention des Urgences Sanitaires (Establishment of prevention and Responses to Health Emergencies)
HAS	Haute Autorité de Santé (High Health Authority)
HCSP	Haut Conseil de Santé Publique (High Council for Public Health)
HIV	Human Immunodeficiency Virus
IGAS	Inspection Générale des Affaires Sociales (General Inspection for Social Affairs)
INCA	Institut National du Cancer (National Cancer Institute)

List of Abbreviations

INPES	Institut National de Prévention et d'Education pour la Santé (National Institute for Health Prevention and Education)
INSERM	Institut National de la Santé et de la Recherche Médicale (National Institute for Health and Medical Research)
InVS	Institut de Veille Sanitaire (Institute for Public Health Surveillance)
IRSN	Institut de Protection Radiologique et Sécurité Nucléaire (Institute for Radiological Protection and Nuclear Safety)
NGAP	Nomenclature générale des actes professionnels (List of professional Acts)
ONIAM	Office National d'Indemnisation des Accidents Médicaux (National Office for Medical Accidents)
TEU	Treaty of European Union
UCSA	Unité de Consultation et de Soins Ambulatoires (Units of Out-patients Consultations and Ambulatory Care)
UE/EU	Union Européenne (European Union)
UHSI	Unité Hospitalière Sécurisée Interrégionale (Secured Interregional Hospital Unit)

List of Abbreviations

General Introduction

Chapter 1. The General Background of the Country

§1. Geography and Climate

1. The French Republic territory is composed of metropolitan France: French mainland and Corsica and the overseas regions: Guadeloupe, Martinique, Réunion, and Mayotte.

France's total land area, with its overseas departments and territories, is 674,843 km^2 (260,558 km2, 0.45% of the total land area on Earth. However, France possesses the second largest Exclusive Economic Zone[1] in the world, covering 11,035,000 km^2 (4,260,637 sq mi), approximately 8% of the total surface of all the EEZs of the world, just behind the United States (11,351,000 km^2 or 4,382,646 sq mi) and ahead of Australia (8,232,000 km^2 or 3,178,393 sq mi).

The European territory of France covers 547,030 km^2 (211,209 sq mi), having the largest area among European Union (EU) members. France possesses a wide variety of landscapes, from coastal plains in the north and west to mountain ranges of the Alps in the south-east, the Massif Central in the south-central and Pyrenees in the south-west.

From south-west to north-east, France shares borders with Spain, Andorra, Monaco, Italy, Switzerland, Germany, Luxembourg, and Belgium.

The north and north-west have a temperate climate, while a combination of maritime influences, latitude and altitude produce a varied climate in the rest of metropolitan France. In the south-east, a Mediterranean climate prevails. In the west, the climate is predominantly oceanic with a high level of rainfall, mild winters and cool to warm summers. Inland the climate becomes more continental with hot, stormy summers, colder winters, and less rain. The climate of the Alps and other mountainous regions is mainly alpine, with the number of days with temperatures below freezing over 150 per year and snow cover lasting for up to six months.

1. EEZ created by Art. 55 of the UN Convention of law of the sea 1982 'The exclusive economic zone is an area beyond and adjacent to the territorial sea, subject to the specific legal regime established in this part under which the rights and jurisdiction of the coastal State and the rights and freedoms of other States are governed by the relevant provisions of this Convention'.

§2. Population

2. On 1 January 2017, the number of people living in France is estimated at 67 million, including 64.8 million in France and 2.1 million in the overseas departments. This figure does not include the 604,400 inhabitants of the overseas communities. In contrast, about 3.5 million people are nationals but not residents in France. We can estimate the number of people with French nationality to over 63 million.

The total fertility rate is 1.93 in 2016, versus 2.9 in 1950 and 1.8 in 1990. The fertility rate is slightly insufficient to replace the population. However, the population continues to increase due to immigration and the increase in life expectancy. In 2016, it stood at 79.3 years for men and 85.4 years for women, up to 10 years in 50 years.

§3. Political and Judicial System

I. Government

3. The French Republic is a *unitary semi-presidential* Republic with strong democratic traditions. The Constitution of the Fifth Republic was approved by *referendum* on 28 September 1958. The executive branch itself has two leaders: the *President of the Republic*, currently *François Hollande*, who is *head of State* and is elected directly by universal adult suffrage for a five-year term and the government, led by the president-appointed *prime minister*.

The French *Parliament* is composed of two chambers, the *National Assembly* (*Assemblée Nationale*) and the *Senate* (*Sénat*). The National Assembly deputies are directly elected for five-year terms. The Assembly has the power to dismiss the cabinet, and thus the majority in the Assembly determine the choice of government. Senators are chosen by an electoral college for six-year terms, and one-half of the seats are submitted to election every three years.

The Senate's legislative powers are limited; in the event of disagreement between the two chambers, the National Assembly has the final say. The government has a strong influence in shaping the agenda of Parliament.

II. Law

A. *Civil System*

4. France uses a *civil legal* system, that is, law arises primarily from written statutes; judges are not to make law, but merely to interpret it (though the amount of judicial interpretation in certain areas makes it equivalent to *case law*). Basic principles of the *rule of law* were laid in the *Napoleonic Code* and must respect the *Declaration of the Rights of Man and of the Citizen* which only prohibit actions detrimental to society.

French law is divided into two principal areas: *private law* and *public law*. Private law includes, in particular, *civil law* and *criminal law*. Public law includes, in particular, *administrative law* and *constitutional law*. However, in practical terms, French law can be divided in three principal areas: civil law, criminal law, and administrative law. Criminal laws can only address the future and not the past (criminal *ex post facto* laws are prohibited). While administrative law is often a subcategory of civil law in many countries, it is completely separated in France. Each body of law is headed by a specific Supreme Court: ordinary courts (which handle criminal and civil litigation) are headed by the *Court of Cassation* and administrative courts are headed by the *Council of State*.

To be applicable, every law must be officially published in the *Journal Officiel de la République Française*.

France neither recognizes *religious law*, nor does it recognize religious beliefs or morality as a motivation for the enactment of prohibitions. Freedom of religion is guaranteed by the constitutional rights set forth in the 1789 *Declaration of the Rights of Man and of the Citizen*. However, since the *1905 French law on the Separation of the Churches and the State*, the State tries to prevent its policymaking from being influenced by religion.

B. The Constitution

5. The Constitution of 4 October 1958 is the founder law of the Fifth Republic.[2] Adopted by referendum on 28 September 1958, it organizes public authorities, defines their roles and relationships. Its Preamble refers directly and explicitly to three other basic texts: the Declaration of the Rights of Man and of the Citizen of 26 August 1789, the Preamble to the Constitution of 27 October 1946 (the Constitution of the Fourth Republic) and the charter of environment in 2004. The last change is the constitutional Law No. 2008–724 of 23 July 2008 on the modernization of the institutions of the Fifth Republic.

The Constitution asserts the primacy of the executive, strengthening the roles of president and government. It guarantees the existence of basic democratic freedoms and confirms its commitment to the Declaration of Human Rights of 1789. The Constitution is at the top of the hierarchy of internal norms. The State is the sole depository of public power, in relationship with decentralized communities. Regions, departments, municipalities, and public institutions of the State are also responsible for ensuring compliance with the general interest and to implement public policies to serve the citizens.

2. www.légifrance.gouv.fr.

Chapter 2. The French Health System

6. France is a centralized country; health institutions[3] depend on a public national structure; the Ministry of Health. Health policy which is defined at the national level by the Directorate General for Health (DGS) is implemented at the local level (regional or departmental). The DGS is responsible for prevention and safety policy, in relation with national health agencies which are, both relays and privileged interlocutors who contribute to the design and implementation of policies which the DGS is responsible for.

Several national agencies were created to meet specific needs. Agencies and the National Authority for Health (HAS), an independent administrative authority, work in coordination, in a structured framework especially around the animation agency system (CASA), which regularly gather their executive directors. Also part of the CASA, the High Council of Public Health (HCSP), the National Institute of Health, and Medical Research (INSERM) and a representative of the executive directors of regional health agencies (ARS).

§1. Ministry of Health and National and Decentralized Institutions

I. The Ministry of Health

7. Since 1930, health was supported by a separate department or was linked to a larger ministry (Social Affairs, Solidarity).[4] It includes several directions:

(a) *The Directorate General for Health*: The Directorate General for Health (DGS) develops and implements policy on the prevention, environmental health, maternity, childhood and specific actions for health, health risk management, and the organization and training of medical and paramedical professions.
(b) *The Directorate* General *for the provision of care*: The Directorate General for the provision of care (DGOS) organizes the programming for the provision of care and hospital investment, for status management and training of the hospital staff, and for the organization of hospital establishments.
(c) *The General* Directorate *for Social Action*: The General Directorate for Social Action (DGAS) directs social action policies in favour of socially disadvantaged groups: adults with disabilities, seniors and families, children, and adolescents. It defines the formation of social professions, their professional and ethical rules. It prepares legislation for the creation and operation of institutions and social and medico-social services. It ensures the rights of users and employees of these institutions and services.

3. *Source:* www.hopital.fr.
4. www.sante.gouv.fr.

II. Other National Structures

8. A-The General Inspectorate for Social Affairs: The General Inspectorate for Social Affairs (IGAS)[5] provides a monitoring and evaluation of the implementation of all public policy in the areas of health, protection and social welfare, labour, employment, and professional training.

B-The High Authority for Health: The High Authority for Health (HAS),[6] established in 2004, is responsible for evaluating the medical utility of all medical acts, benefits and health products covered by health insurance, implementing the certification of health facilities and promoting best practices and the proper use of care among health professionals and the general public.

C-The ANESM: Founded in 2007, the National Agency for the evaluation and the quality of establishments and social and medico-social services (ANESM)[7] sets quality standards for professionals and evaluates the services offered in the social and medico-social institutions.

III. Decentralized Institutions of the Ministry of Health

9. During the decentralizations of 1982–1983, 2004, the powers previously exercised by the State were transferred to local authorities.

A- The regional health agencies:[8] it follows the ARH created in 1996, which are public interest groups between the State and health insurance organizations, whose mission is to define and organize the regional policy for the provision of hospital care, analyse, and coordinate the activities and operation of public and private health institutions. In 2010, they were replaced by regional health agencies (ARS), with extended powers to independent professionals and houses retirement. The ARS, in compliance with the national health policy, are in charge of defining the regional health policy, organization of care, monitoring, and food safety and prevention.

B- Regional and Departmental Directorates for Health and Social Affairs: the regional directorates (Drass) and departmental (Ddass) for health and social affairs are decentralized services of the ministries of Health, Social Action, and Welfare.

The Drass's missions mainly concern: the observation and analysis of social needs, planning, and programming, as well as the allocation of resources dedicated to health care and medico-social spending (excluding skills transferred to ARH).

The Ddass's missions consist of: the implementation of integration policies, insertion and solidarity, the promotion and prevention in public health, guardianship, and control of healthcare and medico-social establishments by delegation of ARH, animation of local actors.

C- The regional conferences on health and autonomy: analyse the specific health needs in the considered population, consistent with the guidelines of the National

5. www.igas.gouv.fr.
6. www.has-sante.fr.
7. www.anesm.sante.gouv.
8. www.ars.sante.fr.

Health Conference. They are involved in the health and medical fields and evaluate the social rights of the user and the equal access to and quality of health care.

IV. The Competencies of the Departments in the Field of Health

10. The 'Conseil Général' (general council) the administrative body of each 'département' has competence for: assistance and social action for older people (Apa), assistance and social action for adults with disabilities (county home for people with disabilities) social assistance to children (ASE), maternal and child health, the fight against exclusion (funds to help the poorest populations and young people ...).

§2. Agencies and Institutes

I. The Biomedicine Agency

11. The Biomedicine Agency (ABM)[9] missions are: medically assisted procreation(MAP) and prenatal and genetic diagnosis, embryo, and embryonic stem cells research and the organ removal and transplantation, tissues, and cells transplantation. In these areas, it evaluates and monitors the therapeutic and biological activities within its competence and participates in the rulemaking.

The agency issues permits for in vitro embryo research and embryonic cells and for the storage of embryonic stem cells for research purposes. It allows the exchange of reproductive cells and embryonic stem cells with third countries for research.

It gives authorizations to multidisciplinary centres for prenatal diagnosis and pre-implantation genetic diagnosis centres, and certification of practitioners of these centres.

It organizes the organ removal and transplantation, manages the National Register of volunteers to donate bone marrow. It promotes the donation of organs, tissues, and cells, as well as the donation of gametes.

II. The National Agency for the Safety of Food, Environment and Labour

12. The The National Agency for the Safety of Food, Environment and Labour (ANSES) ensures human safety in the areas of environment, labour, and food. In addition, it contributes to the protection of the health and welfare of animals, to the

9. Administrative public institution created by the bioethics law of 2004. www.agence-biomedecine.fr.

protection of the health of plant health and to the assessment of nutritional and functional properties of food.[10]

It assesses the risks, provides the competent authorities the necessary scientific and technical support for the development of laws and regulations and risk management. It carries out tasks of monitoring, warning, vigilance, and reference. It proposes to the competent authorities measures to protect public health. In case of serious public health threat, it recommends to these authorities the necessary sanitary measures.

III. National Security Agency of Medicines and Health Products

13. The National Security Agency of Medicines and Health Products (ANSM)[11] was replaced on 1 May 2012 by the French Agency for the Safety of Health Products (AFSSAPS), which it took over the missions, rights, and obligations.

The tasks of the agency are defined in Article L. 5311-1 of the CSP: it is a public institution under the supervision of the Ministry of Health. It guarantees the safety of health products throughout their life cycle, from initial trials to the supervision after marketing authorization.

Its jurisdiction applies to all drugs before and after marketing authorization, to raw materials, derivatives blood medicines, vaccines, homeopathic products, herbal products, and hospital preparations.

Its jurisdiction extends to other healthcare products: organic products and medical devices. Organic products includes organs, tissues, cells used for therapeutic purposes, products of cell and gene therapy, blood components . Medical devices are linked with therapeutic diagnostic, in vitro diagnostic, technical facilities, and medical software.

The agency oversees the cosmetics and tattooing products, and other health products such as biocides and health food products for special medical purposes.

For the EU, it conducts assessments (Article L 5311-2 CSP) and technical control of medicines and health products. The agency monitors the foreseeable adverse effects and may suspend or withdraw a product from the market (Article 5312-1) that becomes dangerous for health.

The agency inspects manufacturing facilities, those of import, distribution, pharmaco-vigilance and those conducting clinical trials (Article L 5313-1 CSP).

The agency issues the following authorizations: placing on the market (AMM) of a product; conduct of clinical trials; temporary authorization for the use (ATU) of a drug, authorization for the importation, prior approval or prohibition of advertising.

10. As a public administrative institution, the National Agency for the Safety of food, environment and work under the supervision of the ministries of health, agriculture, environment, labour and consumption. It was created on 1 Jul. 2010 by the merger of two French health agencies: AFSSA (French Agency for Food Safety) and Afsset (French Agency for the Safety of the environment and labour).

11. 2011–2012 created by Act of 29 Dec. 2011 on the strengthening of the health safety of medicines and health products.

IV. The French Blood Establishment

14. The French Blood Establishment (EFS)[12] organizes the collection of blood and blood transfusion and therapeutic control using blood and its derivatives.

The French Blood Establishment is the guarantor of the safety of the transfusion chain from donor to the recipient. The EFS manages activities: collection, preparation, qualification, distribution of blood products, and provides more than 1,900 health facilities (hospitals and clinics) throughout France. The EFS supplies the French Laboratory of fractioning and Biotechnology (LFB), which manufactures blood derivatives.

V. The High Authority for Health

15. The High Authority for Health (HAS) is an independent public authority with a scientific[13] character, to enhance the quality and sustainability of our health system. It improves the quality of the health system and ensures to all a sustainable and equitable access to care as efficient, safe, and efficient as possible. Implemented on 1 January 2005, the HAS has a legal personality and has a financial autonomy.

The HAS provides advice to assist public decision-making to optimize the collective financial management of devices and reimbursable medical services.

It supports health professionals in the continuous improvement of their clinical practice, defines best practices and proper use of care. The HAS has a network of about 750 visiting experts, authorized to carry out the certification visit of health facilities.

VI. The National Cancer Institute

16. The mission of the National Cancer Institute is to better prevent cancer, to diagnose earlier, ensure access to quality professional care in respect of equity and make innovations and progress more accessible.[14] It finances and implements research activity.

It includes the following dimensions: research, public health, observation, information, provision of health and social care, professional integration. The The National Cancer Institute (INCA) collects information from various data producers to produce a multidisciplinary expertise: risk factors, demographic issues, genetic testing, etc.

The INCA sets standards of good practice and care in oncology, as well as certification criteria for establishments and health professionals in oncology.

---

12. Created on 1 Jan. 2000 with the law that has substantially reorganized the French blood transfusion system, The French Blood Establishment is the only civilian operator of blood transfusion in France. This is a public establishment of industrial and commercial nature, under the supervision of the ministry in charge of health. www.dondusang.net.
13. Created by the Act of 13 Aug. 2004 on health insurance.
14. Established by the Public Health Act of 9 Aug. 2004, as part of the Cancer Plan, to sustain a coordinated national policy to fight against cancer. www.e-cancer.fr.

VII. The Institute for Radiological Protection and Nuclear Safety

17. The Institute for Radiological Protection and Nuclear Safety (IRSN)[15] is the public expert in the area of research and expertise on nuclear and radiological risks.

The mission of the IRSN focuses on the identification of environmental risks, nuclear defence expertise, the prevention of major accidents, the safety of nuclear reactors, factories, laboratories, transportation and waste, and finally human radiological protection (continuous monitoring).

The IRSN defines the programmes of national and international research in its field of competence, contributes to the training and education in radiological protection and nuclear safety. It contributes to the information of the public through publications, the Internet, exhibitions, conferences, etc.

VIII. Public Health France

18. Created by the Decree 2016-523 (27 April 2016), this new public agency (Santé publique France[16]) merges the INVS, the INPES, and the EPRUS.

A. The Institute for Public Health Surveillance

19. The Institute for Public Health Surveillance (InVS)[17] is responsible for monitoring the health of the population, based on a national network of public health. It provides tasks of monitoring, epidemiology, alert and advise public authorities in case of threat or health crisis. www.invs.sante.fr.

Missions of the InVS apply to all areas of public health: infectious diseases; the effects of the environment on the health; risks with a professional origin; chronic diseases and injuries; international and tropical risks.

The InVS provides ongoing monitoring and observation of the health of the population through the collection and processing of data on the health status of the population for epidemiological purposes. The data are collected by the relevant public and private correspondents from the national network of public health.

As part of the health monitoring, the InVS is responsible for gathering and analysing knowledge about health risks, their causes and evolution, studies for each type of risk, the most vulnerable or endangered populations.

---

15. Created by the Act of 9 May 2001 creating a French Agency for Environmental Health Safety and operation was specified by decree of 22 Feb. 2002. The IRSN is a public establishment of an industrial and commercial character placed under the joint supervision of the Ministry of Environment, the Ministry of Industry, Ministry of Research, Ministry of Defence and the Ministry of Health.
16. Santé publique France : www.santepubliquefrance.fr.
17. Created by the Act of 1 Jul. 1998 on the strengthening of health surveillance and monitoring of the safety of products for human use, the InVS has seen its scope complemented and strengthened by the Act of 9 Aug. 2004 on the public health policy to meet the new challenges revealed by the recent health crises and emerging risks.

In case of threat to the health of the population, the InVS promptly inform the Minister for Health and recommends appropriate measures or action. This health warning is intended to prevent the occurrence or mitigate the impact of this threat.

B. *The National Institute for Health Prevention and Education*

20. The National Institute for Prevention and Health Education (INPES)[18] implements the policies of health prevention and education, provided by the public health policy set by the government and Parliament. (Article L 1411-6 of CSP).

This policy aims at improving the health status of the population by preventing the emergence, development or aggravation of diseases or accidents and promoting individual behaviours aiming at reducing the risk of illness and injury.

The law of 9 August 2004 on public health policy has extended the missions to the management of emergency or exceptional situations with collective health consequences by participating in the dissemination of health advices in case of an emergency. The INPES also provides training in health education

C. *The Establishment of Preparedness and Response to Health Emergencies*

21. The The Establishment of Preparedness and Response to Health Emergencies (EPRUS) allows the State to respond to a disaster, emergency or to a serious health threat situation that occur in the country in an efficient and effective manner.[19]

The EPRUS must carry out the tasks related to the preparation of the health system to large-scale health threats. It organizes the health reserve task force: administrative, financial, and operational administration.

It implements response plans to health threats. It ensures the supply of products and the organization of services necessary for the protection of the population faced with health threats – including pandemic.

18. Administrative public institution established by the Law of 4 Mar. 2002 on patients' rights and the quality of the health system.www.inpes.sante.fr.
19. The establishment of preparation and response to health emergencies is a public institution established by the Act of 5 Mar. 2007 and placed under the supervision of the Ministry of Health.

Chapter 3. The Social Security System

22. The social security organization has been created in 1945, by the General de Gaulle's government through the 'ordonnances du 4 et du 19 Octobre 1945'. These orders ('ordonnances') combined all the previous insurances and provided for the principle of a 'management of social security institutions by the parties it concerns'. Since 1946, the social security is included in the French Constitution.

§1. History of the Social Security System

I. Article 1 of the Constitution of 1946

23. 'An organization of Social Security is established for the purpose of protecting workers and their families against all kinds of risks likely to reduce or remove their earning capacity and covering maternity expenses or costs of the family they are supporting.'

Preamble to the Constitution of 1958 concerning social security:

> The Nation shall provide individuals and their families with the necessary conditions for their development. It shall guarantee health protection, material safety, rest and leisure for everyone, particularly children, mothers and elderly workers. Every human being who, because of his/her age, physical or mental state or economic situation, finds himself/herself unable to work, shall have the right to receive appropriate means for living from the community.

II. Evolution of the Social Protection

24. At the beginning, in 1945, the social security has been created for protection against the risks of old age, illnesses, maternity, occupational accidents, family responsibility for trade and industry employees. The social security is funded through compulsory collections from wages. Both employees and employers are contributing. This social protection is based on the principle of social democracy: management by the parties it concerns (joint-management of funds by social partners within an administrative council) and with the principle of expanding the scope to include other population groups.

A. *Three Social Security Funds*

25. They were created in 1967 as well as a Central Agency:

(1) The French National Health Insurance Fund for Salaried Employees (Caisse nationale de l'assurance maladie des travailleurs salariés / CNAMTS).

(2) The French National Old-Age Insurance Fund for Salaried Employees (Caisse nationale d'assurance vieillesse des travailleurs salariés / CNAVTS).
(3) The French National Fund for Family Allowances (Caisse nationale des allocations familiales / CNAF).d) the Central Agency of Social Security Organizations (Agence centrale des organismes de sécurité sociale / ACOSS) ensuring joint-management of the scheme's resources.

B. Universal Health Insurance

26. In 1996, a reform plan was set up, with the aim of creating a 'universal health insurance scheme' enabling the automatic right to social security for 18-year-old and over people who regularly live in France. The plan organizes a control of healthcare expenditure, and a reform of public and private hospital care. Regarding the funding, a new resource is created 'Contribution au Remboursement de la Dette Sociale (CRDS)' applicable to work incomes, replacement incomes, assets incomes, investment incomes and other incomes, such as lottery-style games, horse bets, and casinos.

C. The 'Couverture Médicale Universelle' and 'Protection Universelle Maladie' (the Universal Sickness Protection)

27. In 2000, in order to offer the benefit of social protection to all, creation of the 'Couverture maladie universelle' (CMU), a Universal Health Insurance Coverage., and distribution of the personal Health ID card (Carte Vitale) for 16-year-old and over people.

The particularly worrying financial situation of the Health Insurance system led the government to suggest a structural reform of the system. The law of 13 August 2004 related to health insurance redefines the organization of available health care, is focused on the control of healthcare expenditure, and finally makes changes as far as the CNAMTS' managerial bodies are concerned. (*see* below).

This organization changed with the Article 59 of the 2016 Law of social security finance, that replaces the CMU by the 'Protection Universelle maladie'(PUMa). This is to simplify the access to care for all the persons working or residing in France. Medical care are open to all without any justification. If the person does not work, he or she has to make the evidence of residence on the French territory since 3 months.

The same law allows Health ID card since 12 years old.

§2. Organization of the Social Security

28. Since 1945, Health Insurance has been built on three fundamental principle bases: equality for healthcare access, healthcare quality, and solidarity. Originally established for salaried people and their families, health insurance general scheme has progressively concerned other categories of people, on top of the first category (young people who have already done their military service or do not have to do it, divorced women who do not work, ex-prisoners, and so on).

Thus, health insurance gives anybody the possibility to receive health care according to his/her needs, whatever his/her age and income levels. Today, health insurance guarantees healthcare access for nearly 50 million people.

I. The Different Schemes

29. Health Insurance has three main schemes: the general, the agricultural, and the social scheme for independent professionals:

(1) *The General scheme* covers employees in the industry, business and service sectors, as well as some categories of workers considered as employees. Today, it is the cornerstone of social protection in France since it protects 85% of the French population.
(2) *The Agricultural scheme* (Mutualité sociale agricole / MSA) covers farmers and farm employees.
(3) *The Social scheme for independent professionals* (Régime social des indépendants/ RSI) covers craftspeople, retailers, manufacturers, and independent professions.

The system also includes a number of other special schemes: for sailors and registered sailors, mines, SNCF, RATP, EDF-GDF, Banque de France, Assemblée nationale, Sénat, clerks and solicitor's employees, ministers of religion, and so on.

II. Several Self-Governing Branches

30. The current organization of the social security general scheme comes from the 1967 order which introduces division of social security into self-governing branches: sickness branch, old-age one, family one. All the legislation and the regulation of the social security is collected in the 'Code de la sécurité sociale CSS'.

A. *The Sickness Branch*

31. The French National Health Insurance Fund (Caisse nationale de l'assurance maladie des travailleurs salariés / CNAMTS) manages sickness risks (Article L 321-1 CSS), maternity (L 331-1 CSS), disability (L 341-1 CSS), death (Article L 361-1 CSS) and, with a different management, industrial accidents and occupational diseases (L 411-1 CSS).

At a local level: 101 Local Health Insurance Funds (Caisses primaires d'assurance maladie / CPAM) in metropolitan France and four general social security funds (Caisses générales de sécurité sociale / CGSS) in overseas departments.

At a regional level, in each administrative region: fourteen Funds for Pensions and Occupational Risks (Caisses d'assurance retraite et de la santé au travail/CARSAT) and two Regional Health Insurance Funds (Caisses régionales d'assurance maladie/ CRAM) are involved in prevention and industrial accident and occupational disease pricing.

B. *The Old-Age Branch*

32. The old-age protection (Article L 351-1 CSS) is managed by the National Old-Age Insurance Fund (Caisse nationale d'assurance vieillesse / CNAV) which defines retirement branch thrusts, as far as old-age insurance and widowhood insurance are concerned.

C. *The Family Branch*

33. Family Benefits are defined by Article L 511-1 and following articles of the CSS. The National Child Benefit Fund (Caisse nationale des allocations familiales/ CNAF) manages different social and child benefits.

At the local level, the Child Benefit Funds (Caisse d'allocations familiales/CAF) are responsible for the service related to those benefits: child benefits, family allowance, accommodation allowance, income support, and so on.

D. *The Collection Branch*

34. The Central Agency for Social Security Organizations (Agence centrale des organismes de sécurité sociale/ACOSS) is the national fund of the collection branch of the social security general scheme. It is responsible for social security cash flow management and coordinates the action of the unions responsible for collecting social security contributions and child benefits (Union de recouvrement des cotisations de sécurité sociale et d'allocations familales/URSSAF). At a local level, URSSAFs collect contributions and taxes.

III. The Reform of the System in 2004

35. The law of 13 August 2004 concerning Health Insurance aims at saving health insurance by keeping the universal, compulsory and jointly liable aspects, while fighting against waste and abuse, and acting in order for everybody's effort to lead to a welfare system balance.

A. *Fundamental Principles*

36. Health insurance reform mainly aims at saving health insurance system by consolidating three of its fundamental principles:

(1) *Equal access to treatment*: this must be guaranteed for all citizens, regardless of their place of residence on national territory and income. It assumes the existence of a public and universal health service.
(2) *Quality of treatment*: treatment provided by healthcare professionals is already of high quality, but the quality culture must be developed resolutely in the healthcare sector.

(3) *Solidarity*: everyone must contribute to the health insurance scheme according to their income and receive on the basis of their needs.

While keeping to the fundamental principles reaffirmed in Article L 111-2-1 CSS:

> The Nation shall affirm its commitment to the universal and compulsory character of health insurance, grounded in solidarity. Regardless of a person's age and state of health, every social health insurance policyholder shall benefit from protection against the risk and consequences of health, funded on the basis of his or her resources.

B. Measures Regarding Patients

37.

(1) *Organization of treatment:* to facilitate the coordination of treatment within the healthcare system , the insured person ,over 16 years , chooses a 'referring doctor' .(Article L 162-5-3 CSS).
(2) *Personal medical file* (Article L 161-36-1 CSS): which will contain medical information (allergies, exam results, current treatments, etc.); constituted and updated by the doctor the insured person has chosen, this file will be computerized with respect to very strict confidentiality rules (professional secrecy). The (new) Vitale Card will have a photograph of the insured person and will become an access key to the personal medical file.
(3) *Reimbursement of provided treatment*: a fixed contribution at the policyholder's expenses.

C. Measures Regarding Management

38.

(1) *Reinforcement of control measures* (Article L 114-9 CSS to L 114-22): sick leaves, transport prescriptions, and so on.
(2) *Medication policy*: promotion of generic medicines, ongoing re-evaluation of pharmacopoeia and healthcare standards by the French National Health Authority (Haute Autorité de santé / HAS) (Article L 161-37 CSS to 46).
(3) *Conventional policy* (Article L 162-15 CSS and following articles): a delegation with greater powers, a majority opposition right.
(4) *New organization of management* (Article L 22162 CSS and following articles): reform of CNAMTS' managing bodies, new bodies created within a delegation with greater powers, and changes in the network organization.

Chapter 4. Sources of Medical Law

39. France has a normative system essentially based on written rules, which are based on a hierarchical organization of norms by virtue of which higher norms take precedence over the lower regulations. National sources of health law are made up of all the legal regulations applicable in France. They are comprised of a variety of written norms from international treaties, directives, the Constitution, laws, regulations, decrees, and unwritten standards such as customs and practices. Doctrine and jurisprudence can also be indirect sources of health law. To examine the area of French health law, it is necessary to consider supranational sources (§1) and national sources (§2).

For example, a regulation, a law in the field of public health must always respect the French Constitution. Also, the laws always have to consider the international treaties once these have been ratified.

§1. Supranational Sources

40. The supranational sources in medical law in France are of paramount importance. They are vital to the legislator who must ensure that national laws comply with international agreements and treaties. This implies that the French legislator cannot maintain or vote for provisions opposed to his international commitments. Some of these treaties come from specific bona fide international sources, others from European sources.

I. Bona Fide International Sources: International Treaties

41. In France treaties regularly ratified, and therefore compliant with the Constitution, are incorporated into French law. Moreover, Article 55 of the Constitution[20] anticipates the superiority of ratified treaties over all other norms, notably legislative, subject to the reciprocity of application by the other party or parties. Administrative[21] and judiciary[22] case law has recognized their superiority in text from both before and after.

Many treaties relate to health law. Some are bilateral and others multilateral, and they link France with one or several countries.

42. Thus the *Universal Declaration of Human Rights* adopted by the UN General Assembly on 10 December 1948 in Paris came into force in France the same day. This text recognizes rights which interfere with health law such as the right to human dignity, the right to life, and the prohibition of torture or degrading treatments. It mentions health more expressly as being part of the right to a standard of living in its Article 25:

20. http://www.legifrance.gouv.fr/.
21. CE, 1990, Nicolo, Rec. Lebon, p. 190.
22. C. cass., 1975, Jacques Vabre, D. 1975, 497.

> Everyone has the right to a standard of living adequate for the health and well-being of himself and of his family, including food, clothing, housing and medical care and necessary social services, and the right to security in the event of unemployment, sickness, disability, widowhood, old age or other lack of livelihood in circumstances beyond his control. Motherhood and childhood are entitled to special care and assistance. All children, whether born in or out of wedlock, shall enjoy the same social protection.

This text has laid the international legal foundations of the right to health because since its creation the right to health has been registered in many legally restrictive international and regional treaties relating to human rights.

43. The same is true of the *International Covenants* adopted on 16 December 1966 and which came into force in France on 4 February 1981. This is the *International Convention on Civil and Political Rights*[23] and the *International Covenant on Human Economic, Social and Cultural Rights*.[24] The former Covenant refers indirectly to health law through Article 6 of the right to life and Article 7 on the *Prohibition of Torture and Inhuman or Degrading Treatment or Punishments*. The latter Covenant in its Article 12 more clearly relates to health law. It refers to the right to security and hygiene in the workplace (Article 7), the right to social security (Article 9), the special right to social protection in maternity (Article 10), and the right to benefit from scientific progress and its applications (Article 15). Moreover, it imposes a duty on public authorities to recognize the right of everyone '*to the enjoyment of the highest attainable standard of physical and mental health*' (Article 12). Article 12 also specifies that States Parties must take all necessary measures to assure the best state of mental or physical health for people: 'the provision for the reduction of the stillbirth-rate and of infant mortality and for the healthy development of the child'; 'the improvement of all aspects of environmental and industrial hygiene'; 'the prevention, treatment and control of epidemic, endemic, occupational and other disease'; 'the creation of conditions which would assure to all medical service and medical attention in the event of sickness'.

44. The Convention on the Rights of the Child of 20 November 1989[25] came into force in France on 6 September 1990 which is also a key text in the field of health, particularly relating to children. Article 24 of this Convention stipulates that '*States Parties recognize the right of the child to the enjoyment of the highest attainable standard of health and to facilities for the treatment of illness and rehabilitation of health. States Parties shall strive to ensure that no child is deprived of his or her right of access to such health care services.*' Actions taken by States Parties must therefore aim, among other things, to: reduce mortality among newborn babies and children, assure medical care and necessary health care for them and prohibit traditional practices detrimental to the health of the children. Conscious that the health of the child is closely related to that of the mother, the Convention also asserts that States Parties must additionally assure appropriate prenatal and postnatal care for mothers.

23. http://www.ohchr.org/EN/ProfesionalInterest/Pages/ccpr.aspx.
24. http://www.ohchr.org/EN/ProfesionalInterest/Pages/CESCR.aspx.
25. http://www.ohcr.org/EN/ProfessionalInterest/Pages/CRC.aspx.

45. The International Convention on the Elimination of All Forms of Racial Discrimination (ICERD) adopted by the UN General Assembly on 21 December 1965[26] also relates to the French State from its ratification on 28 July 1971 and its enforcement in national law on 27 August 1971. Article 5 of this text obligates State Parties '*to undertake to prohibit and to eliminate racial discrimination in all its forms and to guarantee the right of everyone, without distinction as to race, color, or national or ethnic origin, to equality before the law*', in the enjoyment of different rights including '*the right to public health, medical care, social security and social service*'.

46. The Convention on the Elimination of all Forms of Discrimination against Women adopted on 18 December 1979[27] and in force since 1980 also constitutes a true 'charter of women's rights'. In ratifying the text in July 1983, France, like other Member States of this Convention, committed to eliminating all discrimination which hinders the access of women to rights in different areas including health. Article 12 of the Convention obligates States Parties, and therefore France, to take all appropriate measures '*to eliminate discrimination against women in the field of health care in order to ensure, on a basis of equality of men and women, access to health care services, including those related to family planning*'. The same article stipulates that States Parties must '*ensure to women appropriate services in connection with pregnancy, confinement and the post-natal period, granting free services where necessary, as well as adequate nutrition during pregnancy and lactation*'.

47. The UN Convention on the Protection of the Rights of all Migrant Workers and Members of their Families[28] of 18 December 1990, which came into force in July 2003, is also an important text relating to health. Its main objective is to protect migrant workers, particularly vulnerable people, from exploitation and the violation of their human rights. Hence Article 28 of this Convention stipulates that:

> Migrant workers and members of their families shall have the right to receive any medical care that is urgently required for the preservation of their life or the avoidance of irreparable harm to their health on the basis of equality of treatment with nationals of the State concerned. Such emergency medical care shall not be refused them by reason of any irregularity with regard to stay or employment.

To date, neither France nor any State of the EU has ratified this Convention. However, it is important to note that this Convention is covered within the Convention on the Rights of Persons with Disabilities.

Apart from the aforementioned texts that mention the right to health directly or indirectly, it seems important to us to mention the international *Convention on the Rights of Persons with Disabilities* adopted by the UN General Assembly on 13 December 2006[29] and which came into force on 3 May 2008. This Convention is far from being only symbolic because States that have ratified its take on certain commitments vis-à-vis the international community in relation to persons with disabilities. This

26. http://www.ohchr.org/EN/ProfessionalInterest/Pages/CERD.aspx.
27. http://www.un.org/womenwatch/daw/cedaw/text/econvention.htm.
28. http://www2.ohchr.org/english/bodies/cmw/cmw.htm.
29. http://www.un.org/disabilities/default.asp?id=259.

Convention constitutes an advance for the recognition of the rights of persons with disabilities. Article 25 of the Convention stipulates that:

> States Parties recognize that persons with disabilities have the right to the enjoyment of the highest attainable standard of health without discrimination on the basis of disability. States Parties shall take all appropriate measures to ensure access for persons with disabilities to health services that are gender-sensitive, including health-related rehabilitation.

Thus, in ratifying the Convention on 18 February 2010, France committed to taking national measures to ensure the basic rights of persons with disabilities. The adoption and effectiveness of these measures will be controlled at international level by a committee of experts.

II. European Sources

A. European Union Health Law Sources

48. The European Union is the heir of the European Economic Community instituted by the Treaty of Rome of 1957 by six founder States including France. Although this treaty is economic, it refers to the right to health notably with regard to the organization of health professions by forbidding any implementation of measures whose nature is to limit the installation of health professionals in Member States and recognition of qualifications between States. Ratified by France, this treaty is part of French national law. This means that it can be cited in French courts. Notably, this is how French courts had to deal with the issue of the illegal practising of medicine.[30]

49. The Treaty on the European Union (TEU) of 7 February 1992, the so-called the treaty of Maastricht,[31] creating the EU, was also ratified by France and therefore integrated into the French legal corpus. The same is true of the treaties of Amsterdam, Nice, and Lisbon.

Without question, since its creation in 1992, the EU has intervened in health matters. Its interventions in the area were intensified with the treaty of Lisbon, which maintains that '*a high level of protection of human health is ensured in the definition and implementation of all politics and actions of the Union*'.[32]

Among EU actions relating to health, the EU strives to ensure that all community policies and actions offer a high level of health protection; help Member States to coordinate their action and to cooperate on health; lead joint action with Member States on threats to health notably as regards serious cross-border threats to health; establish norms and regulations in specific domains such as pharmaceutical products, medical devices, blood products, and organs for transplants. However, EU actions in public health matters only supplement national policies in the area because the area of public health protection is a matter primarily for national jurisdiction. Member

30. Crim. cass, 20 Mar. 1978, Bulletin 104; GP, 12 Jul. 1978, note DO 11.
31. http://www.eurotreaties.com/maastrichtec.pdf.
32. Treaty on the operation of the European Union, title XIV, Art. 168 (ex-art. 152 TCE).

States are entirely responsible for the funding, organization, management, and operation of health services and their national health policies. The EU actions therefore do not replace those of Member States in health matters. National governments are therefore free to organize and provide health services as they wish in accordance with their domestic policies.

Nevertheless, the institutions of the EU can adopt restrictive texts. Such is the case with directives and regulations. Directives are not intended to be integrated into French law immediately but must be included in French law, as with other national laws of EU Member States, within a prescribed deadline, in a way that the French State judges the most appropriate. Directives set targets to be reached within specified deadlines but leave States free in the means used to achieve them. In health law, many directives have been adopted. It is notably the case with the directive of 4 April 2001[33] '*concerning the convergence of legal, regulatory and administrative provisions, of Member States relating to the application of best clinical practices in the management of clinical trials of prescribed medicines*'. This directive was integrated by the law of 9 August 2004. The regulations are directly included in French and Member States' laws, and therefore have restrictive powers.

B. Council of Europe Health Law Sources

50. The Council of Europe has implemented a set of protections of basic rights. Some Conventions set up by the Council of Europe contain provisions, which, without being directly provided for by doctors, apply to medical relation and contentious issues in health. Other conventions directly concern health.

1. Non-health Specific European Conventions

51. It is important to mention first the *European Convention of Human Rights*. Adopted in 1951[34] and ratified by France on 3 May 1974, a Convention that is a primordial text in French law. First, the ECHR can be directly cited in French jurisdictions, which leads the French courts to monitor appliance, even if it opposes a legislative provision. Second, when legal appeal submissions have been exhausted in France, the person subject to trial can appeal to the European Court of Human Rights. In cases of dispute with the ECHR, the French State can be compelled to pay substantial damages in case of refusal to change national legislation or the case law declared as opposed to the Convention. Moreover, the Council of Europe draws up an annual report where the most flagrant national legislation conflicts with the ECHR are shown, implicating the reputation of the Member States concerned. An accumulation of sanctions and bad reputation therefore appear as real incentives that force the States in question to bring their national law into line with the ECHR.

Also, even though the ECHR contains no provisions relating to health, the generality and diversity of recognized rights interfere in the subject area. The ECHR therefore appears as an obvious source[35] of health law. Thus, some ECHR provisions

33. http://www.eortc.be/services/doc/clinical-eu-directive-04-april-01.pdf.
34. http://www.hri.org/docs/ECHR50.html.
35. Van R. Potter, Bioethics, Bridge in the future, Prentice-Hall, Englewood-Cliffs (NJ).

that, without being directly envisaged for doctors, can apply to medical matters. Such is the case with the right to life, provided for in Article 2 of the Convention. This article forbidding intentional death has already been cited in the European Court of Human Rights by a woman who claimed that the right allowed her to demand a right to death.[36] The same article was cited in a French Court to refuse the euthanasia request formulated by a woman suffering from a cancer of the face.[37] It is also the case with the prohibition of inhuman and degrading treatments provided for in Article 3, which allows a person to refuse acts undermining their bodily integrity or dignity. The right to respect for private and family life can also be cited and can be invoked within the framework of medical secrets.

52. It is also necessary to mention *Convention no. 108 on the Protection of Individuals with Regard to Automated Processing of Personal Data*, of 28 January 1981.[38] This Convention constitutes a reference in litigations relating to medical secrets. This is the case in *Z. c / Finland*, where the ECHR Court maintains that national legislation must establish appropriate guarantees to prevent any communication or disclosure of data relating to health which would not comply not only with Article 8 of the ECHR but also with Articles 5, 6, and 9 of the 1981 Convention.[39] In the case in point, it related to disclosure on the occasion of a trial of the seropositivity of the wife of a man accused of rape.

53. The Convention for the Prevention of Torture and Suffering or Inhuman Degrading Treatments of 26 November 1987 can also be cited. This Convention instituting a mechanism of prevention of suffering is exclusively intended for persons deprived of freedom. To monitor the application of this Convention, a committee responsible for undertaking visits to prisons and then writing confidential reports containing recommendations was set up. The work of this committee is of particular importance in the application of health law in the places of deprivation of freedom.

2. European Conventions Specific to Health: The Oviedo Convention

54. To protect people against the danger of new technologies in the field of medicine, *the European Convention on Human Rights and Biomedicine,* also called the Oviedo Convention, was agreed and signed on 4 April 1997.[40] Legal measures and French case law will therefore have to comply with the Oviedo Convention following ratification. This Convention enunciates not only basic principles applicable to medicine but also regarding new technologies in the field of human biology and medicine. The Oviedo Convention contains provisions that refer to, among others, consent, private life, the right to information, genetic tests, medical research, and protection of the embryo. Additional protocols, adopted later, allow every person an explanation to their questions and specification of the applicable rules. To date, France has not yet ratified the Oviedo Convention, but it will soon because its ratification was authorized by

36. CEDH, 29 Apr. 2002, Pretty c. United Kingdom, JCP G 2003, II, 10062, note C. Girault.
37. TGI, Dijon, ord. Ref., 17 Mar. 2008, n° 94/08.
38. http://conventions.coe.int/Treaty/en/Treaties/Html/108.htm.
39. Cour EDH, 25 Feb. 1997, *Z. C/ Finland*, n° 22009/93, Rec. 1997-I, § 95.
40. http://conventions.coe.int/Treaty/EN/Treaties/Html/164.htm.

Article 1 of Law No. 2011–814 of 7 July 2011 relating to bioethics. This will result in legal measures, and French case law will have to comply with the Oviedo Convention.

This being the case, reference to the Oviedo Convention is already taken into account in contentious medical issues before the ECHR Court even before its ratification by Member States. Article 32 of the Oviedo Convention stipulates that '*The European Court of Human Rights, can give advisory opinions on legal questions concerning the interpretation of the present Convention, apart from concrete litigation taking place within a jurisdiction.*' This article has already been implemented in several cases.

55. Thus in the Vo c / *France*[41] case, the ECHR Court provided for the Oviedo Convention as well as the additional protocol carrying prohibitions on the cloning of human beings and the additional protocol relating to biomedical research. The ECHR Court used its influence to show the absence of European consensus on the question of the beginning of life.

Likewise in the *Glass c / United Kingdom*[42] case, the ECHR Court took into account the provisions of the Oviedo Convention in analysing the legal regulations relating to consent to a medical operation. The case concerned the administration of medicine to a child despite the refusal of the mother. The ECHR Court referred to Articles 5–9 of the Oviedo Convention relating notably to consent, to protection of persons incapable of consenting and to emergency situations.

The court also referred to the Oviedo Convention regarding consent in the case of *Bogumil c / Portugal*[43] relating to the surgical operation of a prisoner with a view to extracting sachets of drugs from the stomach.

The Oviedo Convention therefore has an important role in the evaluation of medical litigations. It accredits and legitimizes solutions given by the ECHR Court in health matters.

§2. National Sources

56. French health law consists of a large *corpus* of regulations that do not all have the same binding force. The main sources of French health law (I) and professional sources (II) should be highlighted.

I. The Main Sources of French Health Law

57. The hierarchy of norms, which implies that a lower regulation complies with the higher, is based on fundamental compliance of constitutional sources (A). In this respect, the legal and regulatory sources must stringently conform (B).

41. Cour EDH, Gde Ch., 8 Jul. 2004, *Vo c/ France*, n° 53924/00, Rec. 2004 –VIII §§ 35–38.
42. Cour EDH, 9 Mar. 2004, Glass c/ United Kingdom, n° 61827/00, Rec. 2004-II § 58.
43. Cour EDH, 7 Oct. 2008, Bogumil c/ Portugal, n° 35228/03.

A. Constitutional Sources

58. The reference text in French health law is the French Constitution[44] of 4 October 1958, the founding text of the Fifth Republic. The 'constitutional block' includes the text of the Constitution, and also the Declaration of the Rights of Man and of the Citizen 1789,[45] the Preamble to the Constitution of 27 October 1946, the constitutional principles of and fundamental principles recognized by the laws of the Republic and reaffirmed in the Preamble to the Constitution of 1958.

The French legislature, or in other words, Parliament, consisting of the National Assembly and Senate are required to comply strictly with the provisions of the Constitution when public health texts are drawn up and voted on. Within this obligation, it is all the more fundamental that the Constitutional Council verifies that the adopted resolutions referred to conform to the French Constitution.[46]

Also, the Ombudsman is responsible for ensuring:

> respect for the rights and freedoms by government departments, local authorities, public institutions, as well as any organization involved in public service or for which organic law assigns competence. It can be used by any person feeling aggrieved by the operation of a public service or organization. The matter can be referred to the court directly by himself.[47]

The effective application of constitutional principles, including those relating to public health law, is a national priority. Moreover, French judges, whether through a judicial or administrative order, can apply these texts directly.

59. The Preamble of the French Constitution of 27 October 1946[48] specifies in its first article that:

> in the aftermath of the victory won by the free people over the regimes which tried to enslave and to degrade the human person, the French people one more proclaim that every human being, without discrimination of breed, religion or belief, has inalienable and sacred rights. It solemnly reasserts the rights and freedoms of man and of the citizen sanctioned by the Declaration of Rights of 1789 and the basic principles recognized by the laws of the Republic.

This article is essential since no law, no intervention can 'degrade' the human person, particularly in the area of health law. When the French legislator intervenes, he must comply with this essential provision. Moreover, Article 11 of the Preamble adds that the Nation '*guarantees the protection of health to all, notably children, mothers, and*

44. http://www.legifrance.gouv.fr/Droit-francais/Constitution.
45. http://www.assemblee-nationale.fr/histoire/dudh/1789.asp.
46. On the Constitutional Council: Art. 56 and following of the French Constitution: http://www.legifrance.gouv.fr/html/constitution/constitution2.htm#titre7.
47. On the Ombudsman: Art. 71-1 of the French Constitution. http://www.legifrance.gouv.fr/Droit-francais/Constitution/Constitution-du-4-octobre 1958#ancre2178_0_14_88.
48. http://www.legifrance.gouv.fr/Droit-francais/Constitution/Preambule-de-la-Constitution-du-27-octobre-1946.

older workers'. This constitutional principle expressly states the right of health for everyone, a foundation of public health law. It also specifically mentions the protection of vulnerable persons when it refers to the child, the mother (parturient), and older worker.

60. For international and community health law to be applicable, they must conform to the French Constitution. In extremis, in cases opposing it, the treaty can have no effect on national law. A revision of the Constitution would be necessary for it to be applicable. In such cases, conforming to Article 55 of the Constitution, they benefit from an authority higher than legal and regulatory sourced laws.

B. *Legal and Regulatory Health Law Sources*

61. French health law is distinguished by a variety of its legal and regulatory sources.

1. The Complementarities of Legal and Regulatory Sources

62. The most important health law regulations are included in the legislative parts of the codes, whether it relates to the Public Health Code, the Civil Code, the Social Security Code, the Penal Code, etc. Article 34 of the French Constitution specifies the different areas in which the legislator should intervene. The detail of the law is provided for by decrees of application. Government can also intervene directly by means of prescriptions,[49] provided that they are ratified by Parliament. They are therefore legislative in nature.

In practice, during consultation of the French Public Health Code, reference should be made to legislative articles based on the fundamental principles (L articles.), and there should also be verification that there are complementary provisions in the regulatory part (R articles).

2. The Different Sources in French Health Law

63. The bases of the corpus of regulations in health law are contained in the Public Health Code (2). Other essential regulations are inserted in the Civil Code (1), the Social Security Code (3), and the Penal Code (4).

a. The Civil Code

64. The French Civil Code lays down common law regulations in Family law. In this instance, various essential principles set out the civil rights of the person. Three chapters directly intervene in the area of the health law. The first relates to respect for the human body (Articles 16–16-9) and lays down different public order provisions.[50]

49. Article 38 of the French Constitution: http://www.conseil-constitutionnel.fr/conseil-constitutionnel/francais/la-constitution/la-constitution-du-4-octobre-1958/acces-par-titres.5110.html#titre5.
50. Article 16-9 of the Civil Code.

Where no particular health law exists, judges must refer to this.[51] These essential principles constitute the fundamental basis of French medical law. They are included in many specific Public Health Code provisions organizing medical treatments and research.

65. The first principle is the primacy of the person. By virtue of Article 16 '*the law ensures the primacy of the person, forbids any attack on their dignity and guarantees respect for the human being'*. This principle relates to the protection of the person. The requirement of primacy of the individual must intervene throughout his life, whether at the beginning of life, which goes back to the protection of the embryo, during their life and at the end of their life. It can even go beyond, through, for example, the collection of evidence of the deceased for families during organ removal.

66. The second essential principle regarding the body is non-patrimony.[52] The Civil Code specifies that 'conventions having the effect of conferring a patrimonial value on the human body, on its elements or on its products are null and void'.[53] The principle of the unavailability of the body of the person is a fundamental principle. Article 16-6 of the Civil Code specifies that 'no remuneration can be allocated to one who takes part in an experimentation on his person, removal of elements of his body or in a collection of body parts'. Moreover, 'any convention concerning procreation or surrogacy is null and void'.[54] France only pays expenses incurred during donations of ovules, organ donations or participation in a research operation.

67. The third principle is the protection of the integrity of the person. Article 16-4 stipulates that:

> no one can undermine the integrity of mankind. Any eugenic practices intending the organization of the selection of persons is forbidden. Any intervention aimed at giving rise to a child genetically identical to another person living or dead is also forbidden. Without prejudice to research into the prevention or treatment of genetic diseases, no genetic transformation can be carried out with the intention of changing the derivation of the person.

68. France remains very committed to the protection of the human race. It considerably restrains research likely to change the integrity of mankind. It works on the principle of the future of humanity and the necessity to protect future generations. Besides the general integrity of the person, the legislator also intervenes regarding the protection of the integrity of the human body. Thus, '*no one can undermine the integrity of the human body except in cases of medical necessity for the person or, in the exceptional case of the therapeutic interest of other people'*.[55] This possibility assumes

51. Article 4 of the Civil Code states that '*any judge who refuses to judge under the pretext of silence, obscurity or the insuffisance of the law can be prosecuted for denial of justice'*.
52. Article 16-1 of the Civil Code. In the same sense, refer to Art. 1128 of the Civil Code which stipulates: '*only business related things can be subject to conventions'*. For additional explanation on this text: G. MEMETEAU., ' *Cours de droit médical* '., *supra* , n° 97, p. 96; I. MOINE., ' *Les choses hors commerce; une approche de la personne humaine juridique* '., LGDJ., 1997.
53. Article 16-5 of the Civil Code.
54. Article 16-7 of the Civil Code.
55. Article 16-3 para. 1 of the Civil Code.

the prior agreement of the person following sufficient prior information. Thus, '*the consent of the person concerned must be granted beforehand except in cases where their condition makes a therapeutic intervention not requiring their consent necessary*'.[56] The French legislator lays down the obligation of information and consent of the person across numerous interventions carried out on them, whether in an instance of classical medical treatment during medical assistance in procreation, during organ donation in living persons, the voluntary termination of pregnancy, participation in a research project, and so on. The possibility of not gaining the consent of the person is also sometimes authorized in an emergency, notably when a quick intervention is necessary. The agreement of the person must then be gained as soon as possible afterwards.

69. The fourth and last general principle laid down by the Civil Code in the area of health law is the respect of secrecy, referred to as confidentiality. Article 16-8 provides that:

> no information allowing the identification of either the donor of an element or a body part or the person receiving such can be divulged. The donor cannot know the identity of the receiver, nor the receiver that of the donor. In cases of therapeutic necessity, only the doctors of the donor and of the receiver can have access to information disclosing their identification.

This principle is strongly defended by the French legislator, particularly during the medical assistance in procreation, which can cause difficulties with regard to the right to know one's origins. In this respect, French legislation distinguishes itself from other countries by accepting the lifting of confidentiality in certain cases.

70. The French legislator attaches fundamental importance to compliance with these basic principles. In extremis 'the legislator can prescribe any measures liable to prevent or terminate an illicit attack on the human body or illicit activities concerning elements or body parts, including after death'.[57]

This refers to particular provisions set out in different codes in instances of interventions carried out on the person, whether it is during medical treatments, donations of elements and parts of the human body, research, etc. Often, the provisions for the protection of the person and of their body are accompanied by criminal sanctions in case of non-compliance.

71. Apart from these basic principles, the French legislator provides different provisions on the examination of the genetic features of a person and of the identification of a person by his genetic fingerprint in Article 16-10 to 16-13 of the Civil Code and the use of techniques of cerebral imagery in Article 16-4. Gaining the consent of the person concerned is necessary every time.

Beyond these different special regulations regarding respect for the body of the person, the Civil Code intervenes more generally regarding different regulations of capacity and incapacity of the person, of their representation (Article 371 and thereafter). They have a considerable impact in the domain of French health law, particularly in the Public Health Code where the information and consent of the person constitute a fundamental principal regardless of the medical or experimental treatments acts.

56. Article 16-3 para. 2 of the Civil Code.
57. Article 16-2 of the Civil Code.

b. The Code of Public Health

72. It was created by the Decree of 5 October 1953; it gained a legislative force with the law of 3 April 1958. The 2000–548 regulation of 15 June 2000 gave it its present organization.

73. Initially dedicated to public health for the collective protection of health through hygiene and the fight against epidemics, the code now contains all health/sanitary legislation. Each new law or regulatory text relating to the health field is incorporated into the code, which is regularly updated as well. It includes over 2,300 articles and penal provisions to sanction people or institutions which do not comply with the obligations imposed by the code. As well, the provisions related to overseas territories are included.

Reading the summary gives an idea of the impact of legislation and regulations on the protection of the health of individuals and the organization of medical care activities and prevention. The health code is the main reference to look at when a question is raised about the legal framework of a medical activity.

The articles are numbered by five digits preceded by a letter. The letter L in the legislative part and the letter R is for the regulatory part. The five-digit numbers correspond to the part, book, title, chapter, and section.

The legislative part placed at the beginning contains Article L, from the laws. The so-called regulatory section includes Article R from decrees, orders, and other regulations. The majority of laws passed in Parliament are accompanied by implementing decrees, especially in the field of health care as there are many conditions to be met and practical applications.

Whenever there is an Article L, one shall make sure whether there is a complement in the regulatory part with the corresponding number.

74. The code consists of six parts:

The first part is devoted to the general protection of health, the second part specifically targets the health of the family, the mother and child, and the third part deals with the fight against diseases and addictions. The other parts are related to the organization of health professions (Part 4) Health Products (Part 5), healthcare establishments (Part 6).

Each party ends with the provisions relating to the departments and overseas territories.

Part I: General Protection of Health (Articles L 1111-1 to L 1545-4)

75. Book 1 deals with the protection of people's health, and under Title I with the rights of patients and users of the health system: human rights, information, living will at the end of life, participation of the users in the functioning of the health system. Title II relates to provisions for people who are involved in biomedical research; Title III deals with the examination of genetic characteristics and the profession of genetic counsellor; Title IV provides for compensation of health risks; Title V the risks related to diagnosis and treatment; Title VI of therapeutic patient education; and Title VII prevention of risk factors for health.

Book II organizes the donation and use of human body parts. Following the general principles of Title I, Title II describes the blood donation, Title III the donation of organs, including the donation of gametes.

Book III deals with the links between health and environment, with the '*National agency for safety of food, environment and labor*', for safety of water and food, safety of buildings, swimming pools, radiation, waste management, and toxics vigilance.

Book IV describes the general health administration (institutions, administrations).

Part II: The Health of the Family, the Mother and Child (Articles L 2111-1 to L 2446-3)

76. Book 1 provides for the protection and promotion of maternal and child health whose tasks are assigned to the departmental service for the maternal and child protection. Preventive actions for future spouses and parents, during and after pregnancy, sterilization for contraceptive purposes and medical examination that are mandatory for children are dealt with in this book.

In this book are described provisions for medically assisted reproduction and embryo research and embryonic stem cells, with the related penalties.

Book II deals with the voluntary termination of pregnancy: before the end of the twelfth week of pregnancy and with termination of pregnancy for medical reasons. In the penal provisions are contained both the penalties for illegal abortion and for people who barriers to abortion.

Book III deals with the institutions and organizations, education and family counselling, sex education, homes to care children, and facilities for children and pregnant women.

Part III: Fight against Diseases and Epidemics (Articles L 3111-1 to L 3845-2)

77. Book I organizes the fight against epidemics and certain contagious diseases such as tuberculosis, leprosy, human immunodeficiency virus (HIV) infections. One chapter is devoted to some vaccinations among which some are mandatory. Precautions to take in case of serious health threats with the organization of storage of health products are also planned.

Book II relates to the fight against mental illness, with the organization of psychiatric care, hospitalization requirements at the request of a third party or of the representative of the State and terms reserved for inmates with mental disorders. A chapter is devoted to the rights of the mentally ill, and another for eating disorders.

Book III organizes the fight against alcoholism with the regulation of bars, protected areas, protection of minors, and the repression of public drunkenness.

Book IV describes the treatment of drug addicts who were reported by the health authority or judicial authority and the different conditions for therapeutic injections are described.

Book V organizes the fight against smoking and doping.

Book VI was repealed, he previously dealt with the doping.

Book VII contains provisions about the prevention of sexual offending, the compulsory medical treatment, and socio-judicial surveillance.

Part IV: The Health Professions (Articles L 4001-1 to 4 L 4443–6)

78. The preliminary book specifies the common provisions and conditions of cooperation between health professionals, the representation of health professionals and inter-liberal societies of ambulatory care.

Book I deals with the organization of the medical profession: doctors, dental surgeons, and midwives. There are common dispositions to these professions, special provisions, and penal provisions.

Book II deals with the pharmacy profession, with the monopoly of the pharmacists the professional association (Ordre des pharmaciens), the code of ethics, the profession of pharmacy technician. Since 2017 the profession of medical physicist is defined.

Book III deals with paramedics. There is a wide variety of professions all protected by a degree: nurses, physiotherapists and podiatrists, occupational therapists and psychomotor therapists, speech therapists, orthoptists, and X-ray technicians. Hearing aid specialists, opticians, and dieticians are also included.

For some of these professions, it is important to distinguish acts on prescription and acts under the proper role of these professionals.

Nurse assistants, childcare assistants, and paramedics carry only on medical prescription or under auxiliary control.

Part V: Health Products (Articles L 5111-1 to L 5541–5)

79. Book I deals with pharmaceuticals. The provisions relating to drugs are closely related to the definition of the drug. Pharmacists are involved at all levels of the chain of the drug from the preparation to the distribution.

The provisions apply to medicinal products for human use, advertising, price, pharmacies and pharmacy facilities and inspection of the pharmacy. The other regulated pharmaceutical products are the following: cosmetic poisonous substances, contraceptives, and products causing an abortion. Dietetic foods and tattoo products are regulated in this book. Veterinary drugs are under the law of the pharmacy.

Book II organizes plans of medical devices and their surveillance process. Medical devices of in vitro diagnostics are regulated in the same title, as well as items for children and infants.

Book III describes the powers and duties and organization of the National Security Agency of Medicines and Health Products.

Book IV specifies the penalties.

Part VI: Institutions and Health Services (Articles L 6111-1 to L 6433-1)

80. The first book organizes activities of health facilities: missions, fights against nosocomial infections. The health organization is described specifying the schema of health organization, the conditions for authorization of equipment and heavy materials, emergency medicine and some healthcare services. The general organization of public and private health facilities is specified.

Book II deals with the medical biology: scope, conditions of exercise, organization and accreditation, inspections and sanctions.

Book III regulates emergency medical assistance, medical transportation, telemedicine, and other health services (networks, cosmetic surgery).

c. Employment Code

81. French tradition is marked by the protection of the worker in their relations with the employer in employment contract, governed by private law. This is distinguished from the public framework, which excludes the application of labour law for public civil servants and self-employed persons.[58] Different labour laws provisions have a

58. In this sense, refer to the Preamble of the Constitution of 27 Oct. 1946.

direct link with public health. It also involves the themes of accidents and incapacity at work following an illness or accident, hygiene, risk management, security, maternity, and so on.

82. The worker is protected in view of his illness, accidents, and medical incapacity.[59] For example, the incapacity following an illness or a non-work-related accident, a serious illness, a disability (Article L 2241-5 of the Labour Code), an industrial accident or a work-related illness[60] are all provided for. He or she is protected against risks of exposure to noise (Article L 4431-1 of the Labour Code) risks in mechanical vibrations (Article L 4441-1 of the Labour Code), chemical risks (Article L 4411-1 and following articles of the Labour Code), biological risks and risks of exposure to ionizing radiation (Articles L 4421-1, L 4451-1 to L 4451–2 of the Labour Code). He or she benefits from personal medical supervision when he or she works at night.[61] Committees for hygiene, security, and working conditions,[62] and health services are provided in the workplace (Articles L 4621-1 to L 4625-2 of the Labour Code). Different regulations also relate to health and safety.[63] There are also provisions targeting workers with disabilities.[64]

83. With regard to maternity, measures intervene concerning protection of the pregnancy and maternity, whether during appointment, transfer, dismissal,[65] temporary redeployment,[66] authorized absences, and maternity leave,[67] from loss of prenatal or postnatal employment (Article L 1225-29 of the Labour Code). The same is true for the breastfeeding period (Article L 1225-30 to L 1225-33 of the Labour Code) Other regulations intervene regarding leave for ill children (Article L 1225-61 of the Labour Code) and for parental presence when the child is suffering from an illness, a disability or is victim to an accident of such gravity that a prolonged presence and restrictive care is necessary (Article L 1225-62 of the Public Health Code).

84. Finally, several provisions intervene regarding a health service in the workplace (Article L 4621-1 and following articles of the Labour Code), which shows the advantage of organizing various measures for employees, such as the presence of, for example, a doctor or the activities and facilities of multidisciplinary health teams in the workplace.[68] These professionals intervene notably in case of pathologies linked to job, to work-related accidents and occupational diseases. Certain work categories benefit from specific medical supervision.[69]

d. The Penal Code

59. Article L 1226-1 and following articles of the Labour Code.
60. Article L 1226-6 and following articles of the Labour Code.
61. Article L 3122-42 of the Labour Code.
62. Articles L 2381-1 to L 2381-2, L 4611-1 à L 4614-16 of the Labour Code.
63. Article L 6222-30 to L 6222-32 of the Public Health Code for the contract of apprenticeship.
64. Articles L 5211-1 to L 5215-1, Arts L 6222-37 to L 6222-38 for the contract of apprenticeship.
65. Article L 1225-1 to L 1225-6 of the Labour Code.
66. Article L 1225-7 to L 1225-15 of the Labour Code.
67. Articles L 1226-16 to L 1225-28. of the Labour Code.
68. Articles L 4623-1 to L 4623-8 for the occupational physician and L 4624-1 to L 4624-4 for the multidisciplinary health teams.
69. Article L 4625-1 to L 4625-2 of the Labour Code.

85. French Penal Code is comprised of seven parts among which one directly concerns crimes and offences against the person. Various measures intervene regarding public health. These regulations tend to dissuade the execution of actions risking the protection of the person. They intervene as sanctions only if they harm mankind in general, the person and public health. The punishment of imprisonment and fines are incurred. Penal law has a narrow interpretation (Articles 111-1 to 111-5 of the Penal Code). No one can be punished for a crime or an offence not defined by law. In that respect, only incriminations targeted by the Penal Code and intervening in the area of public health are punished.

86. The Book II of the Penal Code, entitled '*Crimes and offences against the person*', intervenes in respect of crimes against humanity such as genocide noting especially voluntary attacks on life, physical, and psychological integrity and other inhuman acts of similar character intentionally causing significant suffering or serious attacks on physical or psychological integrity (Articles 211-1 and 211-2 of the Penal Code). It also targets crimes against mankind such as the crimes of eugenics and of reproductive cloning.[70] Other measures intervene regarding voluntary and involuntary attacks on the life of a person,[71] voluntary and involuntary attacks in the physical or psychological integrity of the person such as the acts of torture, barbarism, threats,[72] sexual attacks,[73] endangering the person.[74] Specific measures target medical and scientific activities, for example, those relating to experimentation (Article 223-8 to 223-9 of the Penal Code), to illegal termination of pregnancy.[75] Some relate to attacks on the dignity of the person. This is how, for example, discriminations intervene in instances of differentiations take place between individuals because of pregnancy, their physical appearance, their state of health, their disability, genetics, etc. (Article 225-1 to 225-4 of the Penal Code).

87. Different regulations intervene regarding offences in public health, more particularly in the field of the biomedical ethics. They aim at the protection of mankind by punishing the use of cells or of gametes with the intention of creating a child genetically identical to another person, living or dead. It also targets the act, by donation, promise, threat, order, abuse of authority or power, of causing other people to take part in a sample of cells or of gametes, with the intention of giving rise to a child genetically identical to another person living or dead or intervention by propaganda or publicity, regardless of mode, promoting eugenics or of reproductive cloning.[76]

88. Other regulations aim directly at the protection of the human body, particularly at the payment to a person for one of their organs or even acting as an intermediary in order to obtain an organ for payment, or provide such organs of the body of other people. The same is true for the sample of tissues, cells, and elements of the human body and gametes. It also aims at the removal of organs, tissue, cells, and elements of the human body and gametes without the consent of the person. The same is true for

70. Article 214-1 to 214-4 of the Penal Code.
71. Article 221-1 à 221-5-4 for wilful attacks and 221-6 to 221-7 for unintentional attacks.
72. Wilful attacks on the integrity of the person: Arts 222-1 to 222-18-3.
73. Article 222-22 and following of the Penal Code.
74. Article 223-1 to 223-7-1 of the Penal Code.
75. Article 223-10 of the Penal Code.
76. Article 511-1 to 511-1-2 of the Penal Code.

removal, conservation, transformation for scientific reasons, cession, importation, and exportation without compliance with the restrictive conditions set out by the French legislator. The confidentiality of information identifying one or several donors of gametes is also provided for.[77]

89. Different penal measures directly target the protection of the human embryo, notably in cases of payment for such, preceding conception in vitro or the cloning of human embryos for industrial or commercial reasons, research, therapeutic, or non-compliance in respect of restrictive legal requirements and those relating to consent. Other measures intervene regarding embryonic strain cells, in prenatal diagnosis, pre-implantation diagnosis, and MAP.[78]

II. Professional Sources: Best Practices and Recommendations

90. Although professional sources do not have a binding force in the strict sense of the term as they are not issued by the legislator, they are no less essential.[79] Best practices, coming originally from Anglo-Saxon countries and widely applied in the medical field, are developing more and more in French medical and scientific practice. They intervene in the form of recommendations prepared by recognized institutions such as the AFSSAPS[80] to encourage professionals to adopt behaviours assuring them higher efficiency, recognition, and legitimacy in particular areas. Unlike the deontological regulations, they are a priori neither restrictive, nor exhaustive and concern more restricted areas. They contribute only to guide the attitudes of professionals and to suggest proven and accepted practices.

91. They exist particularly in the field of research but can also intervene in medical practices. Such is the case, for example, with best practices drawn up by the AFSSAPS for pharmaceutical preparations targeting preparations carried out in hospital and high street pharmacies, intended for one or more patients where there is no suitable medicine or where the medicine is unavailable. Published in the Official Journal of 21 November 2007, they are considered to be a '*law of opposable reference, intended for high street practitioners and internal health establishment pharmacies to guarantee the quality of their pharmaceutical preparations*'.[81]

The recommendations are an incentive since professional practice regards them very highly. They become all the more important as they are internationally recognized, which is fundamental during medical treatments, particularly in the case of patient mobility or in EU or global research. They can prove to be decisive in the evaluation of the reliability of practices and become imperative for the publication of results in international scientific magazines. They are becoming quasi-compulsory since legislators

77. Article 511-2 to 511-13 of the Penal Code.
78. Article 511-15 to 511-25-1 of the Penal Code.
79. http://extranet.inserm.fr/recherche-clinique-et-en-sante/recherche-sur-les-personnes/aspects-reglementaires/bonnes-pratiques-cliniques-bpc.
80. Replaced by the ANSM since 1 May 2012.
81. http://www.afssaps.fr/Activites/Preparations-hospitalieres/Bonnes-pratiques-de-preparation/(offset)/2#paragraph_8150 For the text of these best practices: http://www.afssaps.fr/var/afssaps_site/storage/original/application/a5d6ae4b3d5fdee013ca463462b7b296.pdf.

are becoming more and more incentive-based. For example, in Article L 1121-3 paragraph 6 of the Public Health Code, it is specified that biomedical research concerning medicines must be carried out in compliance with the regulations of best clinical practices fixed by decision of the French Agency for the Safety of Health Products. For other research, recommendations of best practices are fixed by decision of the French Agency for the Safety of Health Products. This provision is all the more fundamental as it aims at being in compliance with regard to Directive 2005 / 28 /CE of the European Commission of 8 April 2005 fixing principles and detailed guidelines relating to the application of best clinical practices as regards experimental medicine for human usage, as well as requirements for the granting of authorization to make or to import these medicines.[82]

III. Indirect Sources

92. The indirect sources of medical law consist of case law (A), doctrine (B). Although they are not obligatory, they can influence the legislator indirectly when he intervenes in the area of health.

A. Case Law

93. Case law constitutes all the decisions taken by courts and tribunals. It intervenes in all judicial affairs relating to health law in France. It is an indirect source of French medical law since the legislator can draw inspiration from the contents of certain decisions to enact new laws. However, under no circumstances judges can do the same considering that a decision taken in the instance of litigation in the area of medical law constitutes a reference.[83]

The main judgments are prohibited by virtue of the principle of the separation of judicial and legislative powers. Judges are forbidden to carry out judgments on regulation or '*reaching decisions by means of general and regulatory provisions on cases which are submitted to them*'.[84]

94. The French system is based on differentiation between private law and public law. When the judicial judges intervene, whether through higher-level courts, Courts of Appeal or the Court of Cassation, they have to refer to the rules of private law. The same is true in the public sphere, which applies to regulations concerning administrative law organizing relations of patients, public service users of public hospital establishments, and also hospital practitioners with their establishments. The judges of the administrative tribunals, administrative Courts of Appeal, of the Council of State, must refer to public law regulations.

82. *eur-lex.europa.eu/LexUriServ/site/fr/oj/2005/l_091/l_09120050409fr00130019.pdf* also refer to l'*ICH Topic E6* (R1) Guideline for Clinical Practice, Step 5, note for guidance on good clinical practice (CPMP/ICH/135/95), European Medicines Agency, 2002 http://www.emea.europa.eu/pdfs/human/ich/013595en.pdf.

83. Soc. 27 Feb. 1991., Bull. civ. V., n° 102.

84. Article 5 of the Civil Code.

95. Different common law regulations are applicable regardless of the sphere of intervention, whether in private law or public law. For example, regulations relating to the rights of patients are applicable in all medical relations whether they intervene in public hospital establishments or private clinics. The same is true with regulations relating to research and more generally those laid down by the laws of bioethics whether in the donation of human body parts or elements, in MAP, etc. Also, the regulations of criminal law are applicable equally to crimes and offences committed by practitioners intervening privately or by hospital practitioners.

96. The judge must apply the law, as a general rule, in the particular affair he is dealing with, particularly in the area of health law. Under no circumstances can he refuse to apply law at the risk of being punished for denial of justice as laid down by Article 4 of the Civil Code by virtue of which, '*Any judge who refuses to judge, on the pretext of silence, obscurity or inadequacy of law, can be prosecuted for denial of justice.*'

The judge must interpret law. If it is obscure, incomplete or even silent, he can use the preparative texts of law to consider legislative wishes better. Whatever the circumstances, he must always make a decision. For example, he cannot refuse to give a ruling by citing insufficiency of the proof given to him by the relevant parties.[85] Also, in the medical field, he cannot, under any circumstances, refuse to examine a scientific problem, all the more so as it is always possible for him to consult expert opinion beforehand.[86]

B. Doctrine

97. Doctrine is all of the opinions which authors publish in health law. The authors are theoreticians (law and public health teachers), professionals (magistrates, lawyers specialized in health law, doctors, managers of hospital establishments, etc.).

Doctrine is displayed, in general works such as treaties, textbooks, in works specialized in health law, magazines or periodical collections specialized in the field of medical law or sometimes even in more traditional judicial reviews since the area of health is interesting the public more and more, and people are included in debate, included during preparative debates into law by the general States of the bioethics.

Doctrine has a role of information, which is currently important seeing the increasing legislation intervening in the medical field and among decisions taken by tribunals. It particularly has a role of reflexion since it underlines interests, imperfections, and contradictions of law. If necessary, it intervenes through proposals aiming to innovate when there are no specific regulations in a particular area of medical law or to change when some rules seem inadequate or unsuitable. Doctrine works have been particularly important in the bioethics laws whether it is, for example, knowing if it was necessary to allow the practise of surrogate mothers or not, to widen research on the embryo, to increase the number of persons likely to give an organ, etc. In this, doctrine is indeed an indirect source of health law since it can encourage the legislator to react in certain areas.

---

85. Civ. 2nd., 21 Jan. 1993., Bull. civ. II., n° 28; 28 Jun. 2006., Bull. civ. II., n° 174; RTD. Civ., 2006., 821., obs. PERROT.
86. Civ. 1st, 13 Oct. 1981., Bull. civ. I., n° 285.

Part I. The Medical Profession

Chapter 1. Access to Medical Profession

§1. Conditions

98. The practise of medicine in France is organized under three cumulative conditions (Article L 4111-1 of Public Health Code):

(1) Degree, certificate or other qualifications referred to in Article L.
(2) French nationality, citizenship from Andorra or from a Member State of the European Community (Directive 75–362/CEE of 16 June 1975) or from a country party to the Agreement on the European Economic Area, or from a country bound by a settlement agreement with France, from Morocco or from Tunisia. Reciprocal agreements (Article L 4111-3 of the Code of Public Health) allow the installation in France of a specified number of foreign doctors in exchange for an equal number of French doctors in the territory of the other party.
(3) Registration in the List of the College of Physicians, the latter condition is particularly subject to completion of the first two.

A special authorization to practise medicine may be possible by individual order of the Minister of Health.

The registration on the list of the College of Physicians is mandatory for any physician practising on French soil under penalty of prosecution for illegal practise of medicine (Article L 4161-1 of Public Health) penalty: two-year imprisonment and EUR 30,000 fine.

Are exempted from the registration on the roll of the order:

– physicians belonging to the military health service (Article L 4112-6 of the Code of Public Health);
– doctors with the quality of civil servant or staff member of a local public authority who are practising medicine;
– foreign physicians, nationals of a Member State of the European Community performing a service in France (Article L 4112-7 of the Code of Public Health).

§2. Special Situations

99. Attached practitioners or associated assistants are foreign physicians, holders of medical qualifications obtained outside the EU or European Economic Area, who are recruited by public health institutions (Article 11 Decree 2017-326 du 14 mars 2017)). They participate in the activity of the hospital service under the direct responsibility of the physician head of department and can perform medical procedures of general practice. (Article R 6152 -501 and following of the Code of Public Health, Article R 6152-601 and following of Public Health).

The registration authorizes the lawful exercise of the physician throughout the country (Article L 4112-5 of the Code of Public Health). It is delivered by the County Council of the College of Physicians in which the physician establishes his professional residence (Article L 4112-1 of the Code of Public Health).

§3. Registration Procedure

100. Any physician, who applies for registration with the College of Physicians, must submit its request to the Chairman of the County Council.[87] The County Council will appoint a reporter. The Council asks for the communication of the national criminal record of the applicant. It ensures that the applicant meets the requirements of morality, independence and does not have a disability or a condition incompatible with the exercise of the profession (Articles R 4112-2 of the Code of Public Health).

Under Article L 4113-9 Code of Public Health, Physicians who apply for registration on the list must provide the County Council contracts and amendments for the purpose of their practice. The Council provides a list of examples for contracts written with respect to the deontological requirements.

Finally, section L. 4112-2 Code of Public Health states that, the physician who applies for entry in the list must demonstrate sufficient understanding and practise of the French language.

The reporter will meet with the applicant; it is recommended to visit him, to control his or her professional installation.

The County Council should deliver the registration within three months. The refusal should be motivated, and the applicant can appeal the decision to the National Council of Physicians (Article L 4112-4 Code of Public Health).

Once registered on the list of the College of Physicians, the physician must register his degree to the Departmental Directorate of Health and Social Affairs (DDASS) of the place of registration.

All physicians registered on the list must pay a yearly mandatory contribution. The full fee is required for the exercise of the profession. A professional card is delivered by the College of Physicians.

87. Article R 4112-1 and following of Public Health Code.

Chapter 2. The Practise of Medicine

§1. The Code of Medical Ethics 'Code de Déontologie'

101. The term of 'déontologie' is used in France since 1825. The Code of Ethics is developed by the National Council of the College of Physicians and was promulgated as a decree. Since 1947, four versions have been promulgated, the latest on 6 September 1995.[88] Since 2004, the Code of Medical Ethics is included into the regulatory part of the Code of Public Health in Articles R 4127 to R 4127-1-112.[89]

Article 1 defines the scope of the Code of Medical Ethics. The provisions of the code are compulsory to physicians registered with the college, as well as to medical students doing a replacement or to physician assistants. The violation of the duties is sanctioned by the disciplinary jurisdictions of the College of Physicians. Physicians who are not registered with the college are the physicians in the health services of the armies that have their own code of ethics,[90] and physicians serving as medical officers or agents of the local communities who do not exercise medicine.

102. The first title defines *the general duties of physicians* (Articles R 4127-2 to 31) which include the main principles of medical ethics in the form of duties such as respect for life and dignity of the person, non-discrimination, assistance to persons in danger, the protection of the dignity of persons deprived of freedom, respect of confidentiality, and patient choice. The fundamental principles of professional practice are defined: morality and integrity, professional independence, freedom to prescribe, and the duties of training and participating in health education.

Specified are the conditions for implementation of biomedical research, for collection of blood and organ harvesting, and the participation to MAP and pregnancy termination. Finally the last articles are prohibitions. The code forbids: advertising, dichotomy, trickery, overlapping activities, redaction of certificates of convenience, fraud, and abuse of quotation, complicity in the illegal practice, and all behaviour that may discredit the profession.

103. The second title (Articles R 4127-32 to 55) concerning *the duties to patients*, including the elaboration of diagnosis and the prescription, the informed consent,[91] the duties of humanity such as the relief of suffering and the limitation or withdrawal of treatment, and then, the care for vulnerable people such as the end of life, care to patient unable to consent, minors and victims of abuse.

Finally are mentioned the obligations of medical practice: continuity of care, transmission of the record to the patient, the confidentiality sharing with practitioners of health insurance, recommendation to tact and measurement in the determination of fees. Several restrictions are made: no interference in the affairs of the family, no globalization of fees, prohibition of receiving gifts and bequests.

---

88. 5th version after those of 1941, 1947, 1955, 1979. Modified in January 2006.
89. Décret du 29 juillet 2004.
90. Décret 81-60 du 16 janvier 1981.
91. Articles R 4127-35 et 36.

104. The third title (Articles R 4217-56 to 68) focuses on *physician relationship with other physicians* and with members of other health professions. Specified duties ensure a good fellowship and, if necessary, with the help of the College of Physicians Order, find solution in disputes between professionals or with third parties. Several articles deal with how to avoid misappropriation of client or foster relationships with colleagues when the patient consulted another doctor, or following a replacement, or during the hospitalization. Also specified are the conditions to replace a physician, the relationship in the medical team and the relationships with the paramedics. Prohibited are the diversion or attempted diversion of patients, as well as lowering fees for the purpose of competition.

105. The fourth title (Articles R 4127-69 to 108), specifies *the rules of professional practice* First, it discusses the rules common to all types of exercise (Articles R 4127-69 to 84) by recalling that the exercise is personal, and that any physician is able to practise all acts of diagnosis, prevention, and treatment unless it is beyond its competence or experience. The physician must have a proper installation with adequate technical means and ensure the competence of persons who are assisting.

The physician must ensure that persons who assist him are trained on their obligation of confidentiality and comply with them. In the same vein, the physician must protect against all indiscretion medical files whatever the support. Forbidden are the forensic practise of medicine and the exercise under a pseudonym. Several articles deal with references allowed to mention on the professional plates on the door, professional paper for prescriptions, and in directories.

The exercise within a company, a community, an administration must be defined by a written contract that must be communicated to the College of Physicians.

The private practise of medicine is ruled by Articles R 4127-85 to 94 which specify the conditions of installation, of cooperation and association. They must respect the professional independence. The exercise of medicine as an employee, or for control or expertise is also specified.

§2. Practise of Medicine

I. Private Practice and Public Practice

106. Physicians can choose freely to practise liberal medicine in private office, alone or in association with others, or to be employed by a public or a private institution. Currently, freedom of liberal establishment has no limitation even if there are large imbalances in different cities or regions. Several physicians may set up private practice companies according to the rules defined in the Code of Public Health (Article R 4113-1 to Article R 4113-12).

The practice in private institution is subject to the law of private companies. The College of Physicians controls the contract and verifies that medical ethics is respected.

For public institutions, however, the recruitment of physicians is subject to the rules of the public hospital or public local administration that define the terms of competition for admission, the employment status and the disciplinary action.

The Code of Ethics defines the duties which are imposed on physicians in private practice in Articles R 4127-85 to 94. The specific duties of practice as an employee in health facilities are described in sections 116–120.

II. Principle of Free Choice

107. 'The physician must respect the right of every person to freely choose his physician. The physician shall facilitate the exercise of this right.' Article 6 of Code of Medical Ethics.

Until 2005, this free choice had no limits; the patient could go on his own initiative to consult any medical doctor or specialist of his or her choice, in any place whatsoever and receive without restriction the reimbursement by health insurance of the prescribed care.

For the purposes of policy control of healthcare costs, an organization was set up to coordinate care, focused on a physician.[92] Now the physician has got a new function as 'médecin traitant' that has changed relations which existed previously between medical doctor and patient because the 'médecin traitant' coordinates the various interventions of health professionals for the same patient in order to rationalize care.

A. 'Médecin Traitant' and the Care Pathway: 'Parcours de Soins'

108. To appoint his or her 'médecin traitant', the patient is free to choose the family doctor he or she had before, or another general practitioner or specialist, having or not an agreement with the social security, working in private practice or in a public health facility.[93]

There are no geographical constraints. The patient must declare the selected physician to the social security with a special form available on Internet. The declaration must be nominative. It is possible to change the physician without any justification or without the need to notify the previously selected medical doctor.

Compliance to the care pathway is the condition for the patient to have the full reimbursement of the care expenses.

The provisions related to coordinated care pathway apply in healthcare facilities for hospitalizations, consultations, and external acts provided in emergency or not. The health facility ensures that the patient respects the care pathway, by verifying the relevant documents.

The system applies to all insured persons and their dependents over 16 years, including CMUc beneficiaries and patients exempted from 'ticket moderateur' (e.g., 100% reimbursed of their care expenses). Permanent immigrants, holding a vital card, must respect the care pathway.

109. In any case, the patient must have chosen the *médecin traitant* and declared his or her choice to the social security. Otherwise, the patient will be considered out

92. Arrêté du 2 Août 2005 relatif aux missions du médecin traitant salarié.
93. loi du 13 août 2004 relative à l'assurance maladie.

of the care pathways and will have to pay a part of the care expenses that cannot be covered by complementary private insurance.

The patient is considered in the care pathway for any direct consultation with the *médecin traitant,* and for the consultation of another doctor designated as corresponding physician or specialist at the request of the *médecin traitant.*

For a single advice of the corresponding physician, the *medecin traitant* will organize the application of the prescription. But if the intervention of several different specialties is required for the same medical condition, the corresponding physician identifies specialties and consultations in which the patient will have direct access. When the patient respects the plan or treatment protocol, the patient can go directly to the corresponding physician without consulting the *médecin traitant.*

Some exceptions allow direct consultation by the patient outside the above conditions, and do not increase the payment by the patient: when the consultation is motivated by a recognized medical emergency, or performed in a health facility in the following specialties: gynaecology and obstetrics, ophthalmology, psychiatry, neuropsychiatry, or if it is an hospital consultation for tobacco addiction, alcoholism or drug addiction.

In addition, there will be no increase if the patient is out of habitual residence (e.g., holidays), or consults another physician because the *médecin traitant* is unavailable. The physician consulted must make a return of information to the *médecin traitant.*

The patient will not be considered in the care pathway when he or she did not appoint a *médecin traitant* or consult another physician without prescription of the *médecin traitant* out of the above-mentioned situations.

§3. Relationships Between Health Professionals and the Social Security

110. Medical practice is closely related to health insurance, since the entire population residing in the territory can access it due to the principle of solidarity. Payment of care is carried out either directly by the patient who will be partially or completely reimbursed, or by a third party that is to say by an additional private insurance that supports the part which is not financed by the health insurance.

In this system, medical doctors and health professionals organize within an agreement with the social security, the terms of remuneration of the acts and the rate of reimbursement for patients. Even if the rate of acts is fixed, the doctor who chooses to freely set his fees, is placed outside the Convention between Health Professionals and the Social Security , which is quite rare, except for specialties such as cosmetic surgery that are usually not reimbursed by the Social Security..

Relationships between health professionals and the social security are organized within the framework of conventions. The services provided by practitioners who signed the Convention are reimbursed by the social security at a fixed rate; the physician who did not sign the Convention are the exception and the payment of their acts is reimbursed at a very low level and sometimes by a private insurance

I. The Conventions Between Health Professionals and the Social Security

111. The Convention defines two sectors. In sector 1, the physician must respect the fees for medical acts of the general list (Nomenclature) established by the social security, except when the patient has a very special request not included in the nomenclature. In sector 2, the physician freely decides the fees. He must inform the patients the patients by a poster in the waiting room, telling them about his position towards the Convention.

Nevertheless, the principle of the Article R 4127-53 of the Code of Medical Ethics that requires the medical doctor to charge fees with 'tact and moderation' applies. The social security reimburses only the conventional rate. The free fees may be reimbursed by some private supplementary insurance.

112. In 2010,[94] 46.5% of registered doctors in the table of the college of physician exercised in private practice, a total of 99% signed the Convention. A total of 92% of GPs and 40% of specialists practice in sector 1, and 7% of GPs and 40% of specialists practice in sector 2.

A specific case is sector 2 with option of coordinating the 'care pathway'. With this option, physicians involved in the care pathway agree to charge the fee defined by the social security to all acts performed in a medically justified emergency and for children under 16 years. And for technical procedures, they can apply only an additional extra fee limited to 15% of the fee defined by the Nomenclature (NGAP). In addition, they undertake to apply no extra fee and to respect the conventional fee at least in 30% of their business. The physician signs this option for five years, but may terminate the engagement at any time with a notice period of three months.

Only about 500 physicians are practising outside Convention. They are totally free to choose their fees (subject tact and measure) and must follow good medical practices recommended by the HAS. Reimbursement of acts is limited to EUR 0.98, but may open the right to reimbursement by supplementary private insurance according to the contact.

II. New Medical Conventions

113. A new medical Convention was signed on 26 July 2011 with the union of independent medical practitioners. It has three purposes: to give greater access to health care for all, to improve the quality of care and prevention, and to modernize and simplify the conditions of exercise.

Fee-for-service, fundamental principle of private practice persists, but the Convention allows a lump additional compensation under certain circumstances to improve the quality of care. The physician is involved in the prevention, treatment, and monitoring of patients.

A new process has been introduced: the coordination of care in the 'care pathway', and the synthesis of the medical record. The objective is the management and prevention

94. www.leciss.org consulté le 2 mars 2013.

of chronic disease particularly Alzheimer's disease, insulin-treated diabetes, and chronic renal failure.

Incentives have been put in place to improve access to care, to provide a better payment for some care, and to modernize and simplify the conditions for the medical practice.

A. *Strengthening Access to Health Care for Disadvantaged Patients*

114. The third paying policy is generalized for low-income people receiving help for additional insurance who consult a doctor in the framework of the 'healthcare pathways' (corresponding doctor and direct access). The doctor may suggest the third paying policy to patients who are in financial difficulty.

B. *New Forms of Remuneration*

115. Fee-for-service is the base of the remuneration. It is completed with a remuneration package and, from 2012, with a remuneration based on public health objectives. The organization of the office and the quality of service is available to all doctors of all specialties, with the exception of the annual medical summary of the patient for the doctor.

Physicians and specialists in cardiology and in vascular diseases provide the monitoring of chronic diseases and of the efficiency of prescriptions.

With regard to public health priorities, some long and complex clinical activities are especially valued, also by acknowledgment of consultations of high medical value or long and complex: screening for skin cancers, cancers of the cervix; support of psychiatric disorders in children (family counselling), initial management of insulin-treated diabetic patients at the onset of complications; treatment of chronic renal failure by peritoneal dialysis; paediatric monitoring.

1. The Contract for Access to Health Care

116. To encourage doctors to integrate into the 'care pathway', a contract for access to health care is established. In return for the doctor's commitment, personal social security contributions are partially financed by the health insurance.

New payment methods were implemented on 1 July 2013; they value the clinical activity:

- The 'médecin traitant' fee: from July 2013, a special annual fee for each patient is given for the coordination of care. It pays his prevention and monitoring in conjunction with the medical record.
- A lump sum fee of EUR 5 per act for monitoring of elderly people aged 85 or over. This fee values the care of elderly people due to comorbidities of patients and complexity of monitoring their treatment, including the prevention of iatrogenic accidents.
- Increases for some paediatric consultations: consultations for very premature babies and children with serious congenital diseases are increased by EUR 5. An

increase (1 C) for the follow-up consultation after the hospital stay carried out before the end of the first month

- after hospitalization aims at reducing the use of emergency and foster home care.
- For patients with heart failure, this increase is applicable to consultations made within two months following hospitalization.

Technical procedures are also more valued, in particular, surgical procedures (stenting knee, hand surgery, prostate ...) and thirteen specialties are particularly concerned.

The contract provides for an assessment of the quality of service for the purposes of public health. Indicators are: the electronic medical record, the use of prescription management system to optimize the patients monitoring and their support; the computerization to upload and use of e-services and finally providing an annual record.

117. The 2016 Convention, published in the Official Journal of 23 October 2016, makes some changes to the remuneration of medical doctors with increases according to the type of patients (children. elderly people, people with chronic diseases) and according to the proportion of patients benefiting from CMU c. Financial assistance is given for the birth or reception of an adopted child.In order to promote the installation of doctors in areas of low medical density, financial incentives are granted. Funding for telemedicine acts is put in place

Chapter 3. Illegal Practise of Medicine

118. Many health professions have strict rules of professional practice linked in particular to a degree. The illegal practise of such professions is defined in the Public Health Code either when the prescribed legal conditions are not met, or when the health professionals exceed the responsibilities outlined by the rules of competence of their professions, or finally by persons delivering diagnosis or treatment without any diploma.

§1. Medical Professions

119. There are three medical professions in the French law: physicians, dentists, and midwives. These professions are allowed to deliver a diagnosis and to prescribe medicines, which is the monopoly of medical practice. The competence of dentists and midwives is limited to diagnosis and treatment of dental disease for dentists, and monitoring normal pregnancies and practise of normal delivery for midwives. In principle, other health professionals are not qualified to diagnose or prescribe medications.

The illegal practise of medicine is defined by the Article L 4161-1 CSP, of dental surgery by the Article L 4161–2 CSP, and of midwives by the Article L 4161-3 CSP.

The Act of 4 March 2002 extended the powers of certain health professions, allowing for earlier acts under the monopoly of the medical profession thus changing the contour of the illegal practice.

§2. Health Professionals

120. The illegal practices of other health professions are defined in the following articles: Pharmacists (L 4223-1 CSP), Nurses (L 4314-4 CSP), Physiotherapists and Chiropodists (L 4323-4 CSP), Occupational Therapists and Psychomotor (L 4334-1 CSP) Speech Therapists and Orthoptists (L 4344-4 CSP), Pharmacy technicians (L 4243-1 CSP) Laboratory Directors (L 6222-1 CSP) Genetic Counsellors (L 1133-8 CSP), Dieticians (L 4372-1 CSP).

Illegal practise of graduate professionals: even having their diplomas, health professionals can be sued for illegal practice when they perform acts overlapping their competence, or when they do not comply with regulations of the profession: such as practising without registration of their diploma or enrolment to the College of Physicians, during a period of ban.

Some professionals sometimes usurp a title or diploma they do not have. This usurpation is punishable under Article L 4162-1 CSP, regardless of the acts performed with reference to Article 433-17 of the Penal Code: a year in prison and a EUR 15,000 fine.

§3. The Offence of Illegal Practise of Medicine

121. The illegal practice, except the cases already mentioned, is generally the practise of someone claiming to be a therapist, who holds no diploma and is exploiting the gullibility of the people by treating real or imaginary complaints.

It constitutes the illegal practice or medicine to take part usually, even in the presence of a physician, to a diagnosis or treatment of congenital or acquired, real or imagined diseases, by personal actions, oral or written consultations or by any other means whatsoever (Article L 4161-1 CSP).

According to jurisprudence, the diagnosis is the identification of disease after the analysis of symptoms. For example, the examination of a patient in order to locate the lesion is a diagnosis (interpretation of the radio and mechanical diagnosis before providing care Ch Crim April 1987), or the determination of the diseased organ is diagnostic (Cass crim 21 September 2004).

All means of treatment can be sanctioned, palpation or manipulation designed to remedy the pain (Cass crim 5 April 1995), touch of hands that only by his magnetic power is supposed to drive the disease claims (Cass crim 3 December 1953).

122. In the jurisprudence some old decisions sanctioned the Magnetism (1967) Radiesthesia (1957) Hypnotism and Spiritism (1937), Treatment by Plants (1985). More recently chiropractic or spinal manipulation (1978).

Since 2002 the law allows, under conditions, the practise of osteopathy in France and a decision of the Conseil d'Etat in 2007 imposes the publication of legal framework.

The article considers the personal participation of simple personal acts by any means whatsoever is sufficient to characterize the offence; participation includes the concept of complicity: supply of a device (Cass crim 7 March 1973) conducting medical tests (Cass crim 28 May 1957).

As illegal practice is an 'activity' that violates the monopoly, to qualify the offence illegal practice should be a habit, a single act is not sanctioned. Repeating two acts on the same person is sufficient to be qualified as a habit (Cass crim 1971).

§4. Persons Entitled to Carry Out the Civil Suit

123. Because the illegal practice is detrimental to the interests of the medical or health professions, professional associations and professional unions can claim for illegal practice as well as physicians, midwives and dentists, and patients or pretending patients.

§5. Sanctions

124. Two years' imprisonment and a fine of EUR 30,000 (L 4161-5 CSP) are requested for the illegal practise of the medical profession dentist, midwife, pharmacist, nurse, physiotherapist, laboratory director, and a year in prison and EUR 15,000 for the illegal practise of other professions. In addition, the material and equipment may be confiscated, and the prohibition to exercise one or more professions governed by the CSP.

Sanctions for corporate entities are defined by the Article L 4161-6 for the offence of illegal exercise of medical professions and L 4223-1 for pharmacy. The facts must be committed on behalf of the corporation by one of its organs or its representatives. This might be the case of certain sects.

Chapter 4. Control of the Practise of Medicine

125. The medical doctor or the health professional who does not respect its duties or regulations, or infringes the bodily integrity of its patients due to defect acts may be prosecuted and responsibility can be recognized if a fault is proven. The patient who wishes to pursue the professional has the choice of jurisdiction, each action is independent. Since 4 March 2002, France has a compensation system for medical accidents, and the patient can ask a commission (CRCI) for indemnification.

Regarding the professional exercise, special courts sanction behaviours which are contrary to the rules of the profession.

126. The medical profession is regulated by the Public Health Code, which organizes the conditions for exercise and the provisions to control them. It is stated in Article L 4121-2 CSP that the College of Physicians guarantees the professional independence and the compliance of practices to the principles of integrity, honesty, competence, and dedication.

The medical practice is not subject to direct supervision, contrary to the practise of pharmacy which has a staff of inspectors of pharmacy. The control of the College of Physicians is done a posteriori, by the professional courts who sanction the professional rule violations reported to the college.

127. The duties of physicians are defined by the Medical Code of Ethics which applies to all physicians as soon as they enrol in the college. If all the principles of ethics must be respected by every physician whatever the practice, it is mainly private practice which is sanctioned by the professional courts. The physician practising medicine as employees of public institutions are punished under disciplinary status rules of their institution and might be sued by the disciplinary sections of the College of Physicians in a specific condition which are rarely set out.

128. According to Article L 4124-2 CSP, the physicians practising in a public service can be brought to the disciplinary jurisdictions, on the occasion of the acts of their public service only by the Minister for Health, the representative of the State in the department, the Public Prosecutor, or when the violations were performed in a public health service, by the director of the Regional Health Agency (ARS).

§1. Disciplinary Liability

129. The basis for prosecution is the Medical Code of Ethics. Violations of the Code of Ethics are punished by a disciplinary chamber.

Some sections of the Code of Ethics refer as well to obligations imposed by law, and sometimes the same behaviour can be a disciplinary fault and a criminal offence, and judged by the two kinds of jurisdiction, the disciplinary chamber and the criminal court. This is the case of breach of professional secrecy (Article 4127-4 of the R Code of Ethics and Article 226-13 of the Penal Code), the failure to assist persons in danger (Article 9 of the Code of Ethics and Article 4127-9 R 223-6 of the Penal Code) or deliberate provocation of death (Article R 4127-38 of the Code of Ethics and Article 221-1 of the Criminal Code on premeditated murder).

In this case, the proceedings are independent. Article L 4125-5 of the CSP states that 'the exercise of disciplinary action does not obstacle the prosecution that the Public Prosecutor or the individuals may bring in front of the criminal courts in terms of the common law, nor to civil actions for compensation for offence or a tort, nor to special disciplinary proceedings by the administration which employs the physician, nor to a proceeding that may be brought against the physician because of the abuse they are accused of in delivering medical care provided by social laws'.

There is no prescription for disciplinary action, since the legislator did not put any time limit.

Regarding the violations in the relationship with the insured persons, the social security has the power to control the medical activities and the resulting litigation is processed by a special jurisdiction called the section of social security established by the Act of 20 December 1963.

I. The Disciplinary Courts

130. The jurisdictional role of the College of Physicians is exercised through disciplinary chambers in the first instance (regional level) and on appeal at the disciplinary section of the National College of Physicians. This section is headed by a magistrate (Conseiller d'état) from administrative jurisdictions. The legality of the decisions is controlled by the Higher Administrative Court (Conseil d'Etat). These jurisdictions are ruled with the administrative procedure, which is a written procedure.

The disciplinary chambers of first instance are composed of eight members and eight alternates (Article L 4132-7 CSP), and chaired by an administrative magistrate.

The disciplinary chamber of the National College of Physicians has twelve members and twelve alternates, and chaired by an administrative judge appointed by the Minister of Justice. The room sits in formation of at least five members.

II. The Procedure

131. Conciliation by the County Council introduced by the Act of 4 March 2002: when a complaint is received by the County Council, the president invites the plaintiff and the physician to a conciliation board within one month. If conciliation fails, within three months, the Chairman of County Council forwards the complaint to the disciplinary chamber of first instance, with the reasoned opinion of the Council. In some cases, the County Council is associated with the complaint.

132. Submission of the case to the disciplinary chamber of first instance: the case can be submitted by the National College of Physicians, the county councils or medical unions under its jurisdiction, acting on their own initiative in response to complaints. The submission may come from the Minister for Health, the regional prefect (representative of the State) and public health institutions of the region or of the department, (DRASS, the DDASS), the Public Prosecutor or any physician registered on the list of the College of Physicians.

The disciplinary chamber of first instance shall decide within six months of filing the complaint. It may, either on the request of the parties or ex officio order an investigation into the facts relevant to the case. Where appropriate, the minutes of interrogation or hearing are taken.

III. The Hearing

133. No disciplinary punishment may be imposed unless the physician has been heard or called to appear. The jurisdictional decisions have a public character, even if it is decided that the dispute will be discussed in private.

IV. The Sanctions

134. The sanctions are: warning, reprimand, temporary ban (suspended or not), a permanent ban (for salaried public), and the striking off the roll.

After radiation, a special procedure (relèvement d'incapacité) allows the resumption medical practice. After three years, the request is sent to the County Council in which the physician was enrolled at the time of striking off.

As a consequence of the first two sentences: warning or reprimand the physician is deprived of the right to be a member of the County Council, the disciplinary chamber or the disciplinary section of the National College of Physicians for a period of three years. For ban or striking off, denial of right has to be definite. These consequences argue that punished physicians regularly ask to benefit from the amnesty to recover their rights to be elected.

V. The Appeal

135. The appeal decision is possible to the disciplinary chamber of the National College of Physicians within thirty days, which has the effect of suspending the decision. An important innovation was made by the Act of 4 March 2002 which is the opportunity for the complainant to appeal (Article L 4122-3 of the CSP). He may be assisted or represented at the hearing (Article L 4126-2 CSP).

Decisions made by the National disciplinary chamber may confirm the decision of the chamber of first instance, by modifying or reforming the qualification or sanctions, or may cancel it.

Finally, an annulment procedure is possible. The request is presented to the higher administrative jurisdiction 'le Conseil d'Etat'. The request should be made within two months of notification of the decision, and does not suspend the application of the decision.

VI. The Amnesty

136. Sanctions imposed by the disciplinary jurisdictions may be pardoned when in application of an amnesty law (promulgated to each election of the President of the Republic). In this case, the amnesty request is reviewed by the National College of Physicians. The application is admissible within one year after the publication of the law and when the acts were committed in the period of application of the amnesty law. The amnesty is not possible when the behaviour of the punished physician has been contrary to honour and probity. Therefore, when courts impose sanctions, they specify in the decision if the sanctioned facts are contrary to honour or probity. This mention, when an amnesty law is passed, avoids an influx of applications that could be inadmissible.

§2. Liability Resulting of Litigations with the Social Security

137. The so-called contentieux du controle technique organizes the specific disciplinary sanctions for malpractice in providing medical care to insured patients.

I. Basis of the Prosecutions

138. Faults, fraud, and abuse and all malpractice of the medical profession recorded against physicians in care provided to insured persons, are submitted in the first instance to a section of the chamber's disciplinary first instance called 'section des assurances sociales' and on appeal, to the 'section des assurances sociales' of the National College of Physicians. (Article L 145-1 of the Code of Social Security).

The fault is constituted by the breach of an obligation imposed to the physician or to the health professional under a legal instrument. Abuse is an excess of acts regular in the form of prescription but not in the quantity. Fraud is a deliberate act to mislead. The fraud is a criminal offence as well, and can be sanctioned in addition by criminal courts.

The legal texts used as reference to qualify the faults are the rules included in the code de la securité sociale CSS (Code of social security), the Code of Medical Ethics, the Code of Public Health, the agreements of the social security with the professionals, the nomenclature of the medical acts and, more broadly, all texts ruling professional practice or acts performed on insured persons.

II. Jurisdictions

139. The section of Social Insurance of the Chamber Disciplinary of First Instance is a jurisdiction presided over by a member of the Administrative Tribunals or Administrative Court of Appeal. It includes an equal number of assessors' members of the medical and assessors representing the social security bodies.

The Section of Social Insurance National Council of the College of Physicians is chaired by a 'Conseiller d'Etat' (high administrative magistrate); it includes two assessors who are members of the College of Physicians and two members representing the social security bodies.

III. Procedure

A. *Submission*

140. The complaints can be submitted by social security organizations, mutual funds or agricultural social insurance bodies, trade unions of practitioners, for the county councils of College of Physicians concerned, through the Regional Directors of Health and Social Affairs, by the head of department of the regional labour inspection, employment and social policy in agriculture. The physicians' counsellors of various levels of the social security and other schemes of health insurance benefit are entitled to submit cases to the section of social insurance.

The submission can be done separately by the medical service or by the administration of the social security of a credit union, but also jointly, both services have joint their action. The procedure is written and contradictory. The brief includes a statement of the allegations and the arguments that allows the characterization of the fault, fraud or abuse. The findings present the claims of the complainant with a request for sanction or for the refund of the overpayment to the insured person.

In the appendix of the brief, document for evidence are attached; these are care sheets, requests for preliminary agreement compulsory before starting some medical care, written testimony of insured patients, explanations requested to the physician and duplicates of warning letters sent to the physician by the social security.

This brief is addressed to the President of the Section for Social Security. The complaint is notified to the practitioner who addresses a written defence brief within fifteen days. The complainant may respond to the written defence brief by a written brief reply.

IV. The Hearing

141. It stands within eight months of the complaint. The presence of the physician counsellor of the social security is essential. He has to demonstrate the offending acts.

The parties may be represented (Article R 145-20 CSS: social security by a practitioner or a lawyer; the sued physician can be assisted by a colleague or a lawyer). The decision is notified to the parties.

V. The Sanctions

142. They are defined by Article L-145-2 of the Code of Social Security, these are: warning, reprimand, with or without publication, ban temporarily or permanently on the right to give care to the insured persons, with a possible total or partial suspension, and with or without publication. The publication means that the sentence can be displayed in the buildings of the social security accessible to the public.

In addition, the section may request reimbursement to the insured person of the overpayment, or refund the social security bodies of the excess refunded. The deduction may be required even in the absence of any other sanction.

At the end of the suspension of the sentence, if the professional has not been sanctioned again during the suspension by the section of social insurance, the suspended sanction is null and void.

When the sanction of same facts given by the disciplinary chamber differs from the sanction of the section of social insurance, the heaviest penalty applies.

After three years of a definitive ban to care for the insured persons, it is possible to ask for the 'relèvement d'incapacité' as it is possible for the disciplinary sanction.

The prohibition of delivering care to the insured person is applicable for all insured persons, regardless of social protection scheme. The physician cannot give them care free of charge or being replaced by a colleague. He or she must close the office. If he or she continues despite the ban to provide care, it becomes a disciplinary offence and an illegal practise of medicine.

VI. The Appeal

143. The appeal may be made to the social insurance section of the National College of Physicians within thirty days of notification of the decision. It must be accompanied by written reasons. The section of the National Social Insurance Board shall decide all questions of law and fact. On appeal, the aggravation of punishment is possible only if the appellant has motivated the request in that way in the appeal submission.

VII. Cassation

144. The case is presented to the litigation section of the 'Conseil d'état' within two months after the appeal decision. There is no suspension, but a delay of execution of the decision may be requested.

§3. Criminal Liability

145. The Penal Code defines penalties that apply to any citizen who commits an offence. There is no specific offence for medical doctors, so doctor is sanctioned by the general principles of criminal law.

The doctor who is clumsy, reckless or negligent in medical practice may be subject to criminal penalties provided for violations of physical integrity.

Qualification of involuntary injury or homicide can be applied to medical activities that affect the physical integrity. Judges and experts will have to distinguish the criminal act that deserves punishment from non-offending medical accident which is a complication of a medical act performed in accordance with the professional rules.

Other offences may be charged against the doctor in the exercise of his duties as the non-assistance to persons in danger or violation of professional secrecy. In addition, the Public Health Code provides criminal penalties for non-compliance with regulatory requirements.

Sanctions are imposed by the criminal court that hears cases involving offences or the Court of Assizes that hears the most serious offences, such as crimes. These courts impose a personal punishment, imprisonment or a fine, which cannot be paid by an insurance.

Statistics

146. Statistics from the Ministry of Justice does not individualize the offences committed by doctors or health professionals, since they are sanctioned on the same basis as other citizens. Only professional insurance companies have a particular approach of tort actions against physicians. Each year, the MACSF which ensures about half of the practising doctors in France publishes information on it. In 2015, according to the MACSF,[95] on twenty-seven practitioners prosecuted in criminal courts, fourteen were convicted. All practitioners received suspending sentences. This low rate of prosecution could be extrapolated to fifty for all practising doctors in France, and has been quite stable for many years.

Although sanctions are not very numerous, the prosecutions of doctors in the criminal courts are fairly easy since alerting the Public Prosecutor is sufficient. The criminal judge has extensive powers of investigation, and he is the one who gives evidence to qualify the offence.

The victim has the choice of the court before which it will sue the doctor. Preferably to the expensive civil proceedings, the prosecution in criminal courts is chosen for ease of proof and free, especially because, with a specific proceeding called 'partie civile' in a criminal court, the victim may, if the criminal offense is qualified, get in the same judgment compensation for the damage.

I. Conditions for Criminal Responsibility

147. An offence under criminal law is formed by the meeting of three elements: a legal element: article of the Penal Code, a material element by commission of a malpractice (disruptive act, negligence, mistake, carelessness) or omission (non-assistance, lack of supervision, lack of care), and a moral element: mens rea, when the act is committed intentionally or by misconduct.

Criminal offence, personal injury, and the causal link between the two conditions are necessary to qualify criminal offences against the bodily integrity of the person. However, for other offences, it is not necessary that the act or omission has caused damage for the perpetrator to be punished. For example, the disclosure of an information

95. http://www.macsf.fr/vous-informer/responsabilite-professionnel-sante/la-responsabilite-medicale/rapport-activite-risque-professions-sante.html.

held in confidence and that had been collected by the doctor to a third party even if this revelation does not prejudice constitutes a breach of professional secrecy, sanctioned by the Criminal Code.

A. The Criminal Offence (Fault) of the Doctor

148. It will be qualified by the judge who appreciates the elements of the offence that is, under the conditions of implementation of the act or behaviour in question, it will look for a material element, a legal element, an element of intent.

1. The Material Element

149. It can be a malfeasance or an abstention. An act of commission, can be constituted by any medical act or procedure which is causing a damage to body integrity. The Penal Code punishes clumsiness, carelessness, inattention, negligence or any breach of duty of safety or care imposed by law or regulation. We will see later on how the judge retains them in his analysis of case law.

Abstention: the doctor who refuses to move when he is called by a patient who requires care commits the offence of failure to assist a person in danger.

2. The Intentional Element

150. It is the breach of an obligation of safety or prudence imposed by law or regulation. Obligations may be imposed by the Penal Code, but also the Code of Public Health or the Code of Ethics. Several regulations aimed at security especially in acts of anaesthesia, blood transfusion, organ harvesting, and biomedical research. The doctor cannot avoid responsibility by claiming that he did not know the safety rules.

Even if there are no harmful consequences, only the endangered will be punished.

3. The Assessment of Criminal Offence by the Judge

151. The judge assesses the offence 'in concreto' under Article L 121-3 of the Criminal Code, and it will exclude the qualification of misconduct if the offender has followed the normal procedures according to his mission or his functions, skills, and means at his disposal. An expert will inform the judge about the situation in which the offender was and the means he had. (Cass crim 29 June 1999: Bull Crim No. 163, Dalloz, 2000, p. 392 Sleeping obs Y. Mayaud, Gaz Pal 26–27 January 2000 notes from Petit.)

B. Causation

152. The Act of 10 July 2000 distinguishes the offender from those who contributed to its realization when several practitioners contribute to perform the medical act or surveillance. To recognize the criminal responsibility of each of them, the judge will have to establish a definite causal link between the fault and the harmful consequences. For example, for manslaughter, the judge will seek if in the absence of the malpractice the death would have occurred or not. If the death would not have occurred, causal link is established.

153. However the loss of chance of recovery or survival cannot be accepted as the basis for a criminal offence because if the behaviour of the doctor only deprived of a chance of survival this means that there is another cause that contributed to the death, and the causal link is not sufficiently established. (Cass crim 9 January 1979: JCP G 1980, II, 19272, note F Chabas, Cass crim, 7 January and 20 May 1980 D 1981 inf rap, obs J. Penneau; Gaz Palais 1980.2, p. 696). However, if the doctor has created a risk of death preventing any chance or possibility of survival, behaviour constitutes the offence of manslaughter, (9 June 1977 Cass crim Bull Crim 212, JCP G 1978, II, 18839, note Savatier).

The Act of 10 July 2000 establishes in the Article 121-3 of the Penal Code a characterized offence when someone exposes others to the risk of a specific gravity that he or she could not ignore. Indirect causality is recognized when the doctor has created a situation that led to the occurrence of the damage, or he did not take the appropriate measures to avoid the danger (*see* further the offence of endangering others).

The characterized offence was not retained for a surgeon and an anaesthetist charged for manslaughter for a death that occurred after a post-operative renal failure. The doctors had performed exams late and underestimated the severity of the condition of the patient. The court held that they were not aware of creating a danger of a particular importance. However their contractual liability has been held pursuant to Article 470-1 of the Penal Code.

II. Offences Against the Human Person

A. Violence to Life

1. Voluntary Damages

154. The intentional element of the offence is the key point that will distinguish voluntary damages from unintended damages. The intention means that the act was committed voluntarily by a person who wants to harm someone. Case law is very severe, it considers that the intentional element is established when the act was committed intentionally, and the courts do not establish with the will to harm integrity. The Penal Code punishes voluntary acts that let to death.

155. The case of euthanasia: the Code of Medical Ethics, Article 38 prohibits active euthanasia 'The doctor must accompany the dying being until his last moments, by ensuring appropriate care and measures the quality of a life that is ending, safeguard the dignity of the patient and comfort his entourage. He does not have the right to deliberately cause death.'

The act on the end of life organized the provisions on the organization of care at the end of life with the possibility of putting an end to such care without explicitly authorizing euthanasia.

In the Penal Code, there is no specific offence for euthanasia regardless of the author. The lawsuits are based on the general offences of wilful offences. However depending on the circumstances, distinction should be made between passive euthanasia which consists in not delivering the necessary care and let the patient die, and active euthanasia which results in the administration of substances or voluntary actions to cause death.

The voluntary administration of a lethal product in order to put an end to life is qualified as poisoning (Article 221-5 of the Penal Code). It is not necessary that the death is the result of the administration; it is sufficient that the administration has been performed with this intention. The (real or perceived) deadly nature of the administered product is sufficient.

Delivery to a patient of a medicine that the doctor knows that it can cause the death is considered as an intentional act of administration of a lethal product. On the contrary, the administration of contaminated blood could not be qualified as poisoning in the absence of intent to cause death.

Unlike poisoning, whose result is not necessary to qualify the crime, formal intent to kill is required for the qualification of murder (Article 221-1 of the Penal Code), and the evidence of premeditation must be established for a murder assassinate (Article 221-3 of the Penal Code).

The decision from a resuscitator to extubate the patient and stop resuscitation 'which disagrees with all logic and all medical ethics and is contrary to the rules enshrined in the practice' was curiously qualified by the Supreme Court as manslaughter.

Incitement to suicide is punishable under Article 223-13 of the Penal Code. The Penal Code prohibits propaganda or advertising methods to commit a suicide (Article 223-14). The reissue of the book 'Suicide directions for use' justifies the sanction of the publisher (TGI Paris 11 April 1995: JCP 1996 II 22729, note-Gallay Lucas) while the authors (medical doctors) who would not have given their permission are relaxed for the benefit of the doubt.

2. Unintentional Injury to Life

156. Article 221-6 of the Penal Code sanctioning manslaughter defines the act (offence) as, carelessness, inattention, and negligence. The judge must prove not only that the person is deceased as a result of the act but also that the causal link is clear, the simple loss of chance is not sufficient. If the doctor's fault has deprived the patient of any chance of survival, there is a definite causal link between the fault and the death.

Criminal fault that may lead to sanctions are malfeasance in practice: clumsiness or carelessness or fault of omission such as inattention or negligence.

The assessment of the experts will be crucial as they describe the medical acts and procedure and qualify them as careless or clumsy in comparison with the practise of a normally conscientious practitioner. This has been called clumsiness: a fumble lesion of Vater ampulla which led to the spread of bile and pancreatic liquid that cause the death; improper positioning of the patient on the operating table causing abdominal compression impeding the normal flow of the brain causing a shock responsible for death.

These were described as recklessness: the fact for an anaesthetist to leave prematurely the bedside of a patient after surgery, which is a fault having a causal relationship with the death or having poorly positioned forceps obliging the obstetrician to conduct strong and repeated pulls on the foetus resulting in the death of the mother.

A negligent act includes the lack of verification of the emptiness of the stomach or of the control blood group; the lack of verification of a dressing despite the complaints of the patient causing a gangrene; forgetting clips is qualified as inattention in involuntary injuries.

B. Damage to the Integrity of the Person

1. Voluntary Damage, Violence

157. A very old decision related to the sterilization performed at the request of male patients, is a voluntary violence, and the consent of the 'victims' cannot justify the offence.

Body modifications of transsexuals may be punishable under Article 222-91 of the Penal Code for deliberate violence that led to a mutilation. But without any modification of the criminal law, the Code of Medical Ethics in Article 41 states that 'no mutilating intervention can be performed without serious medical reason, and unless emergency or impossibility without information from the interested person and without her consent'.

Medical justification may be for psychological reasons related to the great moral distress of transsexuals. By allowing the change of civil status of a transsexual after a treatment leading to a change in the appearance of a transsexual, the Cour de Cassation implicitly recognized the legality of the surgery.

Practising a tubal ligation at the time of a childbirth without the consent of the patient could constitute a deliberate criminal offence. But as ligation causes a reversible sterility, the offence constitutes an offence and not a crime. (Cass. crim. 19 January 2005, No. 03-87210).

2. Unintentional Damage to the Integrity of the Person

158. Article 222-19 of the Penal Code:

> Causing, by mistake, carelessness, inattention, negligence or breach of a duty of safety or care imposed by Law or regulation, a total incapacity to work for more than three months is punishable by two years of imprisonment and by a 30,000 euro fine. In case of a deliberate breach of duty of safety or care imposed by law or regulation, the penalties are increased to three years of imprisonment and to 45,000 euros fine.

Article 222-20 of the Penal Code:

Causing, by mistake, carelessness, negligence or breach of duty of safety or prudence imposed by law or regulation, a total inability to work up to three months, is punishable by one year of imprisonment and by a 15,000 euros fine.

3. Administration of Harmful Substances

159. Article 222-15 punishes 'The administration of harmful substances that impaired physical or mental integrity of others.' To be qualified as such, the offence requires knowledge of the hazardous nature of the substance and excludes dosing errors or manipulation. (Cass crim 10 May 1972: D.1972, p. 733, note DS).

4. Doping

160. Article L 232-10 of the Code of Sport prohibits to any person to prescribe, administer, apply to sports without medical reasons, doping substances. The penalty is of five-year imprisonment and a fine of EUR 75,000 (Article L 232-26 of the Code of Sport). The sanction is for the person who prescribes, not for the person who uses doping.

III. Offences Committed During Certain Medical Procedures Performed on Patients

A. Endangering the Life of an Individual

1. Risks Caused to Others

161. The new Penal Code wanted to punish dangerous behaviours that could be encountered in the field of road safety or work. The Article 223-1 punishes exposure to a very serious risk of death or injury that can cause a mutilation or permanent disability by the manifestly deliberate breach of an obligation of safety or care imposed by law or regulation. This text applies to physicians when they are under an obligation of a particular security defined by the Code of Public Health such as safety in anaesthesia or blood transfusion safety.

The material element of the offence consists of a breach of obligation relying on the professional. The article does not sanction a general duty of care but a specific provision. The fact that the doctor fails to comply with his professional duties under Articles R 4127-32 and R 4127-33 of the Code of Public Health: obligation to provide care to the patient with conscience and attention and use of the best process to elaborate the diagnosis is not sufficient to constitute the offence of endangering the life of others because they do not impose specific safety obligation. (Cass. crim., 18 March 2008, No. 07-83067, No. 1623 FS-P + F).

The intentional element can be realized by a simple inattention; the violation must be clearly deliberate; it means that the doctor is aware of the obligation that relies on him, and that despite this, he does not respect it. Safety health professionals are fully aware of their obligations.

2. Failure to Rescue

162. Article 223-6 of the Penal Code prescribes five-year imprisonment and a EUR 75,000 fine, for anyone who wilfully fails to bring to a person in danger assistance that, without risk to himself or to others, he can give, either by his personal action or by causing help. This article reproduces the terms of former Article 63 of the Penal Code, which was directed to any person in the presence of a person in danger. But it was applied mainly to sanction doctors, and the former case law is very abundant: a doctor, knowing that a newborn baby was in danger because of his illegal birth but had a significant chance of survival (Cass crim 23 June 1955.), a doctor who is aware of very critical symptoms, refusing to examine the patient and takes action without effect on the infectious process that he deliberately refused to diagnose, (26 March 1997 Bull Crim crim 123: D 1999. Somm; Penneau 384 obs) a surgeon on duty informed by a call that a car accident injured patient was headed to the hospital and required his presence, refuses to move while he was aware of the risk faced by the patient (Tr. corr Draguignan, 28 January 1983: D 1983 IR 400).

The Code of Medical Ethics imposes an equivalent obligation in Article 9; the doctor is required to provide assistance or trigger off the appropriate rescue.

For a long time, for fear of prosecution, doctors went to the bedside because it is the mere refusal to move which constitutes the offence; the development and the organization of emergency care with paramedics have limited situations where patients were left without assistance.

The case law does not define the concept of risk regardless of the cause or circumstances of occurrence; it is sufficient that the doctor is alerted of a person in danger. In addition, if the risk is finally not realized, it does not excuse the denial of assistance. It is up to the doctor to evaluate the seriousness of the risk and assess it. If no element allows the doctors to diagnose a situation that threatens the patient's life, he will be acquitted. (Nancy, 17 June 2004: JCP 2005.IV.1956).

The doctor is not asked to overcome the danger, even if the condition is so severe that medical action will not bring any rescue; only assistance is required.

The Triggering Off Emergency Care

163. The offence is qualified for the doctor who did not trigger off emergency care and contented to discharge himself from his obligation by advising parents to go to the hospital without having to call ambulance or the hospital to prepare the arrival of the child (Cass crim 4 February 1998: Dr pen.1998, p. 96 obs M. Veron, D.1999, somm.p. 384 obs.J.Penneau)

B. Other Offences Involving Patients

1. Experiments on the Human Person without Consent

164. Performing or having performed on a person biomedical research without obtaining the free, informed, and express consent of the person concerned (Article 223-8 CP) is punished for a three-year imprisonment and a 45,000 euros fine.

The same penalties are applicable when biomedical research is performed while the consent has been withdrawn.

The Criminal Chamber of the Cour de Cassation upheld the sanction against a doctor who conducted research on a very weak and vulnerable patient and obviously unable to give free, informed and express consent (Crim 24 fevr.2009: bull crim No. 45, D. 2009.2087, note Delage).

2. Offences Related to Pregnancy

165. A sanction is provided in the code of public health for propaganda, advertising or provocation in favour of abortion (Article L 2221-1 of the CSP). The provocation to legal abortion is punishable even though there was no abortion performed.

Illegal Abortion

166. In 1975, the French Parliament passed an act allowing abortion (*see* special section IVG) putting a partial end to criminal prosecution for abortion. In 1993, these provisions were permanently repealed. Only performing an abortion without the consent is punished by the Criminal Code (Article 223-10 CSP). This provision deals with the situation of a single minor woman on which abortion is performed with the consent of the holder of parental authority, but without getting, as required by law, the consent of the applicant.

In contrast, the Public Health Code provides penalties for the practise of abortion without complying with the obligations set up by law (Article L 2222-3 CSP) or to provide the woman with the material means to practise abortion on herself. The Court of Appeal of Paris held that the judge has to determine whether the assessment made of the serious danger justifying therapeutic abortion was justified. The experts appointed by the court established that abortions were carried out on the basis of forged certificates issued by two doctors who had the qualifications to deliver them.

IV. Other Offences in the Professional Practice

A. Breach of Professional Secrecy Special Paragraph

167. Special section p. 106

Respect of the professional secrecy for the doctors and the healthcare professionals, is a deontological and legal obligation. The obligation of confidentiality is imposed on all professionals who are thereby led to know the elements of privacy and all information relating to the person and his or her family. Any secret information brought to the attention of professionals is protected, and the disclosure is punished under the Article 226-13 of the Penal Code.

B. Forged Documents

168. The production of forged documents exposes the doctor to sanctions under Article 441-1 of the Penal Code. Article 441-7 specifically deals with the forgery related to medical practice such as a document or a certificate stating materially incorrect facts or falsification of a document or certificate originally sincere or use of a document or falsified certificate.

Penalties are increased to three-year imprisonment and a fine of EUR 45,000 when the offence is committed for the purpose of prejudicing the Treasury of the State or the heritage of others.

C. Breach to Respect for Human Body after Death

169. Autopsy or practise of organ harvesting outside the conditions laid down by the law can be described as violation of the integrity of the corpse (Article 225-17).

§4. No-Fault System of Indemnification

170. The law 2002–303 du 4 mars 202 has set up a no-fault indemnification system for medical accidents based on two entities: the ONIAM and the CCIs. The ONIAM is a National Compensation Office for Medical Accidents, Iatrogenic Diseases and Nosocomial Infections, and the compensation procedure is organized by the conciliation and compensation commissions CCIs.[96]

I. The ONIAM: Missions, Administrative and Financial Organization

A. Missions

171. The National Compensation Office for Medical Accidents, Iatrogenic Diseases and Nosocomial Infections (ONIAM) is a public institution of the State, in charge of compensation, under the national solidarity, of the damage caused by the occurrence of a medical accident, iatrogenic disease or a nosocomial infection (L1142-22.CSP).

The ONIAM is also in charge of repairing the damage due to a mandatory vaccination (L.3111-9), or resulting from infection with HIV (L.3122-1), and the hepatitis C caused by blood transfusion or injection of blood products (L. 1221-14).

96. The name of the commissions has been changed by the Law 2009-526 Art. 12 . The CRCI ' Commision regionales de conciliation et d'indemnisation ', are named now Commissions de Conciliation et d'Indemnisation. CCI.

The office is also in charge of facilitating and, where appropriate, proceeding with the settlement of disputes relating to damage caused by benfluorex.

The obligations of the Association France-Pituitary arising from its role in organizing the treatment of patients by the growth hormone between 1973 and 1988 are transferred to the ONIAM.

B. Administrative Organization

172. Two councils are involved in the functioning of the ONIAM: the 'Conseil d'Administration CA' the (Board of Directors) and the 'Conseil d'orientation' (Advisory Council).

The Conseil d'administration (CA) includes, in addition to its Chairman (appointed for three years, renewable once), one-half of State representatives, and one-half of qualified persons and representatives of users, professionals and health institutions, representative of insurance companies and the staff of the ONIAM. These charges are performed free of wages (R1142-46 CSP). The members of the CA and the staff of the ONIAM are bound by professional secrecy (226-13 and 226-14 of the Criminal Code). The CA shall establish general principles concerning the offers of compensation by the office; it also discusses the administrative and financial matters such as rules of procedure, budget and financial accounts, contracts, offers of compensation and transactions.

The 'Conseil d'orientation (CO)' is chaired by the Chairman of the CA of the ONIAM. It counts twelve members including three representatives of the users of healthcare services. The members of the CO are subject to a declaration of interest (L. 1142-24-3) published on the ONIAM website. (R1142-47 CSP).

The CO meets at least twice a year. A quorum of half of the members is required. It may proceed to hear expert or any person or authority that could enable it to clarify its guidelines (R1142-50 CSP). *(It may call an expert or any authority that could enable it to clarify its line of conduit/guidelines)*

The CO addresses (R1142-51 CSP): the investigation of cases, the rules on expertise safeguarding, the principle of independence and contradictory support for victims, and the development of guidelines on the legal framework for transactions and references for indemnification.

C. Financial Organization (Article L1142-23 CSP)

173. Obligations of the ONIAM shall consist in the payment of compensations to victims, the cost of administrative management of the ONIAM and of the regional commissions and the costs of medical evaluations.

The resources of the ONIAM come from a general grant paid by health insurance organizations; a grant paid by the State in compensation for vaccination accidents, and consequential damages to prevention, and a grant paid by the French Blood Establishment in compensation for post-transfusion hepatitis.

II. The CCI Composition and Functioning (Article L1142-5 CSP)

174. In each region, one or more Commission for Conciliation and Compensation (CCI) is responsible for facilitating the settlement of disputes relating to medical accidents, iatrogenic diseases and to nosocomial infections, as well as other disputes between users and health professionals, health institutions, health services or agencies and producers of health products referred to in Articles L 1142-1 and L 1142-2. For conciliation, the commission may delegate all or any of its powers to one of its members or to one or more external mediators.

The Commission is chaired by a judge in business or an honorary magistrate (Article L 1142-6 CSP). The Commission includes representatives of patients and users of the health system, health professionals, and heads of establishments and health services, as well as members representing the ONIAM and the insurance companies.

All CCI members and those who assist them are bound by professional secrecy (Article 226-13 and 226-14 of the Criminal Code).

A. Composition (Article R 1142-5 CSP)

175. Each CCI has a president and twenty members: six representatives of users, two health professionals in private practice including a physician, a hospital practitioner, a manager of public health establishment and two managers of private health facilities, the representative of the President of the Board and of the Director of ONIAM, two representatives of insurance of civil liability, four persons qualified in the compensation for injury. The commission members are appointed for a term of three years, renewable (Article R 1142-6 CSP).

The Commission can deliberate only if at least seven members are present (Article R 1142-9 CSP).

Prevention of conflicts of interest: Members of the committee and mediators must declare, when they have a direct or an indirect, family, professional or financial links with people whose applications are examined. Or any link with health professionals, health facilities, services and health agencies or producers, operators and distributors of health products, involved in this request (Article L 1142-6 CSP).

B. The Conditions for Compensation by the CCI

1. Degree of Seriousness

176. In order to be compensable by the CCI under national solidarity principle, the damages must reach a level of physical or mental permanent impairment over 24% (Article D 1142-1 CSP).

The same degree of seriousness is accepted in two cases: for a temporary suspension to work or the temporary disability due to a functional deficit equal or over 50% incapacity for more than six months.

Exceptionally, characteristics of seriousness can be recognized in two other cases where the victim is permanently incapable of performing his professional activity, or when he or she has particularly serious problems, including economic ones and difficulties in living conditions.

To assess whether the damage have the characteristics of seriousness defined by the commission, one or more experts are appointed. The parties are informed of the identity and qualifications of the expert (Article R 1142-14 CSP).

There is a sliding scale for evaluating disability rate for victims of medical accidents, iatrogenic diseases or nosocomial infections (Article D 1142-2 CSP). If the scale does not provide the rate, the expert may conduct the evaluation from other references but has to inform the CCI of the references used (Article 3 D 1142-CSP) to complete its mission.

When the committee considers that the damage does not have the character of seriousness under section II of Article L 1142-1, it declares itself incompetent. Then there is a possibility of conciliation (Article R 1142-15 CSP).

2. Settlement Procedure

177. The CCI may be seized by anyone considering himself or herself wronged for damage attributable to an activity for the prevention, diagnosis or treatment, or by his legal representative, or by the beneficiaries of a deceased person (Article L 1142-7 CSP). The person informs the CRCI of court proceedings in progress related to the same facts. If legal claim in justice is brought, the person shall notify the judge of the recourse to the commission.

The actions in justice are prescribed by ten years from the consolidation of the damage (Article L 1142-28 CSP).

When damages have the characteristics of gravity required by the commission, the commission delivers an opinion on the circumstances, causes, nature, and extent of the damage, medical and on the compensation scheme applicable. The opinion of the CCI is issued within six months (Article L 1142-8 CSP).

In addition, when the damage is the result of a nosocomial infection, the commission reports this nosocomial infection to the general director of the regional agency for health and to the ONIAM.

When a medical accident partly results of a malpractice in the contested acts, the CCI specifies which part of damage can be liable to the physician or the establishment, and which part to be compensated under the ONIAM no-fault basis (Article L 1142-18 CSP).

3. Modalities of Settlement

178. The claim is presented with a specific form sent by mail to the CCI in whose jurisdiction the medical act was carried out. The Article L 1142-7 provides a list of documents to support the claim that includes a medical certificate stating the damage and any document necessary to establish that the damage has the degree of seriousness over 24% (Article R 1142-13 CSP).

The CCI will inform of this claim to the professional, the establishment or healthcare organization which must indicate to the commission the references of the insurer that guarantees their civil liability.

4. Panel of Experts (Article L 1142-12 CSP)

179. The CCI will appoint a panel of experts selected from the national list of experts in medical accidents. The Commission establishes the expert mission, ensures the acceptance, and determines the period within which the expert's report must be submitted. The commission has to immediately inform the ONIAM of this mission.

As part of its mission, the panel of experts or the expert may conduct such investigation and ask the parties or any third parties to provide any relevant document. The transmission of these documents is carried out without any limitation due to medical or professional confidentiality. The experts are bound by professional secrecy (Article 226-13 and 226-14 of the Criminal Code).

The panel of experts or the expert ensures the contradictory nature of the expertise, which are attended by the parties. The parties can be assisted by a person or persons of their choice. The panel of experts or the expert takes into account the submissions of the parties and shall, upon request, join to report all relevant documents. The expert can take the initiative to seek the opinion of another professional. The ONIAM supports the cost of expert missions.

5. Hearing of the CCI (Article R 1142-16 CSP)

180. When the commission receives the expert report, it sets the date for meeting. The parties are heard at their request or at the request of the commission. They may be assisted or represented by a person of their choice. The commission may hear the expert or the panel it designates.

The opinion of the committee specifies for each kind of damage on the circumstances, causes, nature, and extent of damage and its assessment of the liabilities incurred. It indicates if the damage meets the requirements provided for in Article L 1142-1-1, and if, on the date it is made, the status of the victim is permanently stabilized or not.

6. Opinion of the CCI

181. The opinion is sent by registered mail with return receipt to the applicant, the ONIAM, the professional, the facility, the healthcare organization questioned by the claimant and to its insurer (Article R1142-17 CSP).

Where the opinion indicates that the damage involves the responsibility of several persons, it is sent to each person considered and to their respective insurers. The opinion is also sent to the medical department of social security where is or was affiliated the victim when the damage occurred, as well as to the other third party that paid care expenses for the damage.

Where appropriate, the commission shall forward its decision to the insurer or ONIAM with the expert report and all documents submitted by the applicant to enable them to make an offer. The medical information is transmitted in respect of medical confidentiality.

7. Conciliation

182. The Commission assembled in its conciliation composition examines applications for litigation (Article R 1142-20 CSP): an application for conciliation is sent by registered letter, mentioning the name and address of the applicant, those of professional, institution, centre or healthcare service or producer, operator or distributor of health products in question, and the subject of the dispute.

The Commission shall hear the interested parties to the dispute and attempts to reconcile them. If full or partial conciliation is achieved, the Commission establishes the terms of conciliation in a conciliation document. This document also shows the points of disagreement when the balance is partial. The document is signed by the parties and the commission Chairman or his representative. A copy of the conciliation document is delivered or sent to each concerned party (R1142-22 CSP)

8. Divestiture

183. If it is conducive to resolve the dispute and with the consent of the applicant, the Chairman of the commission may divest himself of the application for conciliation and transmit to the Commission of the Relations of Users and Quality of care concerned or at the County Council of College of Physicians, dentists or midwives, or, if appropriate, the concerned regional council or central council of the National Order of Pharmacists (Article R 1142-21 CSP).

9. Delegation

184. The Conciliation Commission may delegate the conciliation mission to one of its members or to one or more independent mediators who offer a guarantee of competence and independence (Article R1142-23 CSP).

Part II. The Physician-Patient Relationship

General Description

185. In the countries of southern Europe, the physician-patient relationship is often presented as paternalistic with imbalance in favour of the physician. This situation has changed in the last twenty years in France. Gradually the patients' rights emerged in the different legislations, and were incorporated into new articles of the Code of Medical Ethics. Subsequently, under the pressure of patient associations, special laws guaranteeing their rights were enacted.

Chapter 1. The Doctor-Patient Relationship and the Respect of Patient Rights

§1. The Duties of the Physician in the Code of Medical Ethics

186. Since 1955, the Code of Medical Ethics defines the duties of doctors to patients. Over the updates (1979 and 1995) and through new articles, the code identifies more and more protection of the rights of patients. The physician must act in the interests of patients.

The fundamental principles of medicine are considered in the code as general duties. Traditionally medical ethics requires respect for human life and of the dignity of the person (Article 2); the obligation to provide assistance to the endangered person or to ensure that the patient receives the necessary care (Article 9).

Protecting the confidentiality of information on the patient requires the physician to respect professional secrecy (Article 4) and recommends not to interfere in the privacy of the patient (Article 51).

It took until the 1995 updated version to incorporate into the Code of Ethics, the requirements of the contract of care such as the information (Article 35) and the consent (Article 36). (*See* special section p. 57) Previously, only the Article 8 of the code allowed considering the patient's wishes 'as much as possible'. While the jurisprudence of the civil courts had since 1936 established the basis of the relationship of care between the patient and the physician as a contract, there was no obligation to consent in the Civil Code. The 1994 law on respect for the human body amended the Civil Code and requires an informed consent to allow the doctor to impair bodily integrity.

187. Article 35 of the Code of Medical Ethics defines the terms of the information that the doctor must give the patient '… honest, clear and appropriate to the patient's condition, and to the investigations and treatment the physician offers …' Nevertheless, the physician has the possibility to leave the patient in the ignorance of serious diagnosis or prognosis serious, the physician appreciates the situation 'in all conscience'.

Article 36 provides that the consent of the person treated or examined must be sought in all cases and allows the patient to refuse the investigations or treatments available. This is an important step forward for the rights of patients who want to exercise their autonomy.

188. However the right of patients sometimes collides with the obligation to save human life that weighs on every physician. Administrative case law has ruled, recognizing both that non-compliance with the will of Jehovah's Witnesses patient who was transfused against their will is a fault, but however, this fault cannot be a source of liability.

The obligation to relieve suffering (Article 37) and to accompany the dying person with safeguarding his or her dignity (Article 38) completes the respect due to the patient.

The physician must respect the rights of patients. The physician must respect the right of any person to freely choose his or her physician. The latter should facilitate the exercise of this right. (Article 6 of Code of Medical Ethics).

The physician always accompanied the patient for the allocation of social benefits (Article 50) or for establishing the materiality of medical findings by writing medical certificates. (Article 76 of the Code of Medical Ethics)

189. For the subject deprived of freedom (*see* special chapter), the physician has the right to alert the judicial authorities of any abuse recorded (only when the subject consents, unless it is a minor). The physician must not endorse by his mere presence violations of the physical, mental integrity, or dignity (Article 10).

§2. The Emergence of Patients' Rights in Health Legislation

190. Health legislation which governs the medical activities is also protective of the rights of patients.

I. The Laws Governing Medical Activities

191. We can consider that the first decisive law to enforce patients' rights is the law on termination of pregnancy (1975). It is over thirty years, Mrs Simone Weil has presented the first law that recognizes the woman in distress (without defining the conditions for assessing the distress), the right to terminate her pregnancy. Many protests have been raised during the parliamentary debates, which now seem so displaced, such as the risk that such a law would expose the birth rate. Therefore, the application of the law was temporary for five years to see the consequences on nativity and has revised in 1979 to a definite law.

192. The law allowing organ procurement in 1976 was motivated by the benefit of patients waiting for transplantation. The interest of third parties justified the infringement of bodily integrity. In establishing the principle of a presumption of consent, the legislator obliged the person to voluntary object removing of organs (by any means including the record in a register). It is unclear that the public is well informed of this right, despite frequent media campaigns.

193. Since 1978, the Data Protection Act regulates the creation of medical records and defines the conditions governing access for the subject to the data collected so that he or she can safeguard his or her private life.

Legislation protecting persons who consent to biomedical research (1988) has set up the terms of consent and associated guarantees for subjects that are much more binding when the subject receives no direct personal benefit from the research.

The legislator convened in 1994 the conditions governing access to medical assistance for procreation in prenatal diagnosis, analysis of genetic characteristics and the use of human body parts).

The Code of Medical Ethics in September 1995 has integrated different laws: Article 15 for biomedical research, organ harvesting in Article 16, the use of reproductive techniques in Article 17, and termination of pregnancy in Article 18.

II. The Laws on the Organization of Care

194. Access to health care for all citizens (equity principle) is defined in the Hospital Act of 1970 which states the mission of public service to welcome any patient who needs care. The principle of continuity of public service requires institutions to ensure continuity of care and to organize transfers of patients to the most suitable facilities to meet their needs. In private practice, Article 47 of the Code of Medical Ethics obliges the physician at all times to ensure continuity of care.

In the changes of the Hospital Law in 1991, the rights of patients has been placed in the foreground with the free choice of care facility (public or private), the transmission of the medical file to the patient through the intermediary of a physician and the management of pain.

195. The 'ordonnance' of 24 April 1996 first created a commission of conciliation for patients to inform the users of the public healthcare service to assert their rights, and second, appointed representatives of patients on boards of governors (Conseil d'administration) of public hospitals.

Fight against pain is one of the concerns of the National Agency for accreditation of healthcare facilities. During the evaluation, indicators of pain relief are taken into account as well as the access to palliative care.

III. The Physician as Advocate for Patients' Rights

196. As a repository of information relating to patient's health, the physician must inform the patient of the consequences, for him or her, of the dissemination of medical information he or she may have.

A. The Physician as a Guarantee of the Confidentiality and Privacy

197. The right to privacy has for a long time been defined in France by the Article 9 of the Civil Code: 'everyone has the right to respect for privacy'. The elements of privacy that must be kept secret are linked to the personality of the individual: the health status, information regarding family and home.

The physician must respect the secrecy of personal information; he has a duty of confidentiality. The breach of confidentiality or invasion of privacy is achieved by the interference of any third party without permission of the subject. The consequences are compensated by the civil justice for the damage caused. The physician is also likely for disciplinary action if he violates section 51du Code of Medical Ethics. Breach of confidence is also punishable by the law. The disclosure of secret information is punishable by the Penal Code in Article 226-13 and 226-14. This obligation of confidentiality is general and absolute, and in the French law, the subject itself cannot allow anyone to reveal the information protected by the law.

B. The Medical Guarantees in the Analysis of Medical Genetic Characteristics

198. Law 94-653 of 29 July 1994 introduced in the Civil Code the Article 16-10, which states that genetic analysis can be performed only for medical or scientific purpose, requiring obtaining the informed consent of the person. For research purposes, the genetic analysis is carried out with informed consent in writing as required by the so-called Huriet-Serusclat law.

The examination of genetic characteristics for medical purposes can be made only if there are symptoms to confirm or refute a genetic disease. If there are no symptoms of genetic disease, only a limited list of genetic anomalies can be searched. A free and informed consent on the scope of the examination must be expressed in writing, after an individual medical consultation: genetic counselling.

The results are presented and discussed with the applicant in a clear and appropriate consultation. The physician must respect the patient's right to decline hearing the result and must, in this case, mention their refusal in the file. Exceptionally, in the interest of the patient, the physician appreciates the opportunity not to give the result.

C. The Contributions of the Law of 4 March 2002

199. The legislator has transposed the obligations weighing on the physician to rights of the patient. The law also recognizes new rights to patients. Under the umbrella of health democracy, the rights of the patient are clarified and expanded.

Thus, any user of the health service has the right to protect his or her health by all available means (Article L 1110-2). The patient is entitled to respect for his or her dignity (Article L 1110-2), the respect for personal information (Article L 1110-4). The patient should not be subject to discrimination in access to prevention and health care (Article L 110-3 1). Appropriate health care should be provided and one must grant him or her proper care and treatment whose effectiveness is recognized and security guaranteed (Article L 1110-5).

1. The Patient's Information

200. Everyone has the right to be informed of his health condition. This information includes, treatments or preventive measures that are proposed, their usefulness, their degree of urgency, their consequences and the risks normally predictable frequent or severe that they have and the alternatives. In case of care refusal, the patient must be informed of likely consequences.

Information is delivered in a face-to-face interview. The will of a person to be kept in ignorance of a serious diagnosis or prognosis must be respected except when third parties are at risk of contamination.

The patient's information on his health condition is expanded; it also covers the cost of care in order to facilitate the participation in the decision.

2. Direct Access to Medical Records

201. The law allows access to all the information held by health professionals. The accessible information is the formalized documents that have contributed to the monitoring of diagnosis and treatment, the written exchanges between health professionals (except the information collected from third parties not intervening in the therapeutic management).

Access to the file can be done directly or through a physician. The presence of a third person may be recommended by the physician when the patient reads the file. Rights holders have access (Article L 1111-7) to the information necessary to understand the causes of death, to defend the memory of the deceased or to assert their personal rights.

3. The Appointment of a Person of Trust

202. The person of trust has been established by Article L 1111-6 of the Public Health Code. This person will be consulted when the patient becomes unable to express his or her wishes: any adult may designate in writing a parent or a close person or a physician. This designation may be revoked at any time.

All these provisions are intended to strengthen the autonomy of the subject and undermine the image of the paternalistic doctor-patient relationship.

D. The New Relationship Between Physician and Patient

203. In addition to patients' rights, the law has established bonds that generate patient accountability.

1. The Autonomous Patient: Responsibility of the Users of the Health System

204. Given the information and recommendations provided, every patient makes decisions regarding his or her health, together with the health professional. Therefore, patients should also receive information on therapeutic alternatives. A time for thinking is provided and the consultation of a third party is possible for advice, so that the patient can participate in the choice of therapy.

The person has acquired the right to refuse care regardless of circumstances. While legislation on palliative care only allowed the refusal of the alternative care in end of life, the Act of 4 March allows the patient to refuse any type of care. This denial must be accepted after providing information and included in the file.

205. A limit persists which is the endangerment of the life of the patient. Some physicians refuse to leave their dying patient alone without care. The law on end of life care can respect the wishes of the patient, to oppose any resuscitation. The patient may even argue his choices by the expression of living wills.

2. The Rights That Patients Cannot Exercise by Themselves

206. Some people are more vulnerable than others and require special protection from the parents, physician or society. Their wishes must be respected when they are expressed. The physician guarantees respect for all human beings and protects their health and their rights. When the person is unable to express his or her wishes, no intervention or investigation can be performed, except in an emergency or impossibility, without the consultation of a trustworthy person or a family member or a close person.

Regarding information and care for children, since the Act of 4 March 2002, minors are entitled to receive their own information and to participate in decision-making concerning them in ways appropriate to their maturity (Article L 1111-2 CSP).

The legislator has even introduced an exception to Article 371-2 of the Civil Code, which provides the physician to obtain the consent of the holder of parental authority in case the minor objects to the consultation of the owner to keep secret about their state of health (Article L 1111-5 CSP). To be supported in decision-making, the minor may be accompanied by an adult of his choice.

207. A kind of 'social' autonomy is even recognized by minors in certain cases: when a minor whose family ties are broken receives the benefit of CMU, the consent of the parent is not necessary, only consent of the minor is required.

In all circumstances, the minor's consent/assent must be systematically sought if he is able to express his will and to participate in the decision-making. (Article L 1111-6).

Access to the medical file is exercised by the holder of parental authority. At the request of the minor, this access takes place through a doctor (Article L 1111-5).

3. Patients' Rights and Interests of Third Parties

208. The interest of the patient governs relations between physicians and patients. When the physician has to make choices for his or her patient unless the latter can consent, the physician should provide the medical acts in accordance with the principle of beneficence in the best interests of the patient.

But the interest of third parties or society sometimes justifies actions or interventions on the human body or on elements of private life. For a long time, the principle of organ donation was well accepted by all, the interest of the receiver justifying the organ transplantation. But there is now a need to develop new researches for private or commercial purposes with biological material. In both the cases, such violations of the bodily integrity are allowed for the needs of third parties.

a. Use of Biological Samples

209. For medical research, fragments of tissue are collected in care institutions with a variety of biological samples and medical data associated with it. Those samples, often collected from surgery on fragments of human tissues to be destroyed, do not affect the integrity of the person.

Nevertheless when samples are linked with identification information, they deserve protection and respect and the person from whom they come must be informed of the use of the material.

The patient is informed of the harvesting of biological samples and may object to the use for research or for any secondary use. When samples are stored in bio banks for genetic research, the written consent of the person is required.

b. Exchanges of Data and Medical Records

210. Some studies require large sample collections and associated data. Cross-border exchanges are allowed within the EU by directive. In France, the Law 94-548 of 1 July 1994 allows the transmission of medical data protected by professional secrecy to researchers provided as far as the patient is informed that he or she may exercise a right of opposition. Care teams are not constrained to follow these requirements for the studies conducted on the patients from their services.

An advisory committee on the processing of medical data has been created to give an opinion on the research methodology the relevance, prior to authorization of the CNIL.

Pharmacogenomics studies are conducted on this type of collection. Professionals and industrial companies seek medical teams to provide databases to advance research faster. In that case, the interest of the scientific community will prevail. Regarding possible commercial uses, the availability of these data raises the question of remuneration, which is not organized by the regulation.

Chapter 2. The Physician-Patient Relationship in Specific Terms

211. The physician who provides a medical act has a duty to inform the patient in order to obtain the consent to the act or the informed refusal. The rights and autonomy that patients are claiming in managing more their health are therefore faced with the obligations of physicians. The medical decision engages the moral and professional liability of practitioners.

In September 1995, the Code of Medical Ethics introduced the requirement of informed consent to the physician, whereas before, he was merely asked to respect the wishes and the wills of the patient as far as possible. Thus the Code of Medical Ethics began to comply with the civil jurisprudence of the contract for care, and with Article 16-3 of the Civil Code, on respect for the human body set up by the law of July 1994, which says: '*The integrity of the human body can be infringed only in cases of medical necessity ... the consent must be obtained before ....*' The term of medical necessity has been replaced in July 1999 to that of therapeutic necessity.[97]

§1. Information and Consent in the Code of Medical Ethics

212. The updated version of the Code of Medical Ethics of 5 September 1995 included these obligations in Articles 35 and 36. The requirement for information and obtaining consent applies to all physicians regardless of their place of practice in public or private establishments because physicians practising in public hospitals are required to exercise with respect for professional ethics.

Article 35 of the Code of Medical Ethics:

> The physician must provide a fairly clear and appropriate information to the person that he examines cares or advises about his health condition, the investigations and treatment offered; throughout the disease, the physician respects the personality of the patient in his explanations and make sure of their understanding.

Article 36 of the Code of Medical Ethics:

> The consent of the patient for must be obtained in all cases. When the patient able to express his will, is refusing investigations or treatment, the physician must respect the refusal after having informed the patient of the consequences.

These articles are applicable to competent patients, able to give a valid consent. In the case of incapacity for minors or incompetent persons protected by the law, the Article 42 states that, in the necessity of care the physician should alert the parents or the legal representative of the patient for obtaining the consent. In case of emergency, even without parents' consent or representative's consent, the physician should provide the

97. Act n° 99-641 du 27 juillet 1999.

necessary care. When the assent of the incompetent person can be obtained, the physician should take it into consideration as far as possible.

I. A Specific Condition for Minors

213. The Article 11 of the Law 2002-303 of March 2002 introduced the Article L 1111-5 in the Public Health Code which is derogation for the consent procedure for care on minors in some circumstances. When the treatment or the surgery is necessary for the safeguard of the health of a minor, if the minor expressly refuses to inform one or two parents and wishes to protect the secret of his or her health status, the physician is allowed to perform care without the parent's consent. Therefore, the physician must first try to convince the minor to inform the parents, and if the minor maintains his or her refusal, the treatment or the surgery can be realized on the minor accompanied by an adult person of his or her choice.

When a minor who does not have any more links with his or her family and receives the 'Couverture maladie Universelle CMU',[98] assistance provided by the social security, the consent of this minor will be sufficient.

§2. Lack of Information in Court Decisions

I. The Burden of Proof of Information in Civil Jurisprudence

214. Since the duty to inform is now an obligation for the physician, the Supreme Court changed its jurisprudence in 1997, applying to the physician the burden of proof, in application of the general principle for any debtor of an obligation to provide the evidence of its execution. The burden of proof of the lack of information which previously rested with the complainant now relies on the physician.

A. The Cousin/Hedreuil Decision

215. The decision of 25 February 1997[99] caused great excitement in the medical world: a patient undergoes a colonoscopy with polypectomy, during the latter intestinal perforation occurs. An action for damages was brought against the physician and the clinic. The patient pleads the lack of information about the consequences of the act.

In accordance with an established jurisprudence, the Court of Appeal of Rennes had held that the burden of proof rested with the patient. But the Cour de Cassation breaks decision of the Court of Appeal. This was a major shift in jurisprudence by reversing the burden of proof, saying 'who is legally or contractually bound to a

98. The CMU is a special protection set up by the Law 99-641 du 27 juillet 1999 for any person residing in France since three months who has not health insurance and very low incomes.
99. arrêt Cousin/Hedreuil du 25 février 1997 Gazette du Palais 1997-1-274.

particular obligation of information must prove the execution of that obligation'.[100] This reversal of the burden of proof has caused some emotion among physicians which has been concerned to seek appropriate means to provide such proof, and to define the content.

B. The Following Decisions

216. They have contributed to precise the modalities of the evidence and the content of the information to be given.

In October 1997, the Cour de Cassation stated that the evidence could be provided by any means:[101]

> The physician has the burden of proving that he has given to the patient information fair, clear and appropriate on the risks of investigations or care that it offers in order to enable the patient to give consent or informed refusal. This duty to inform weighs both the prescribing physician and on the one who performs on the prescription and the evidence of this information may be made by any means.'

The following year, two decisions stated:[102]

> that except in cases of emergency, inability or refusal of the patient to be informed, a physician must give a clear and honest information on all the severe risks associated with investigations and treatments available and the physician is not exempted of such information by the mere fact that such a risk is realized only in exceptional circumstances.

About the content, it was clarified also in the decision of 27 May 1998[103] which says that:

> the information must include not only the serious risks of care and investigations proposed by the physician, but also those linked to the treatment requested by the patient. The physician cannot hide behind the choice of the patient, when this choice exposes to an undue or disproportionate risk.

It shall be understood as serious risks, the possible occurrence of fatal, debilitating or serious aesthetic consequences.

100. This obligation applies to all professional debtors of an obligation of information or counselling: attorneys, sollicitors, insurance agents.
101. Arrêt du 14 octobre 1997 Guyomar JCP 1997 II 22942.
102. arrêts du 7 octobre 1998 Bull Cass Civ I n° 287 et n° 291; JCP 1998 G II 10179 Cl Sainte Rose et note Sargos.
103. ' Renversement de la charge de la preuve de l'information donnée au malade par le gastrentérologue ' Revue de la société 'endoscopie digestive 1997.

II. The Information in the Administrative Jurisprudence

217. The information obligation which weights upon public hospitals is defined by Article L 1112-1 of the Code of Public Health as follows:

> In compliance with the rules of professional conduct applicable to them, practitioners in public institutions provide information to care receivers. The paramedical personnel participates in this information in its field of competence and the respect of own professional rules.

As a result, the administrative courts have qualified the lack of information as 'faute de service' only when the hospital did not deliver information on known risks.[104] Administrative jurisprudence has remained stable and did not qualify the fault for the failure to inform of the rare or exceptional risk,[105] or of serious risks when the act is motivated by the medical status of the patient.[106]

The decision of 5 January 2000: following embolization for arteriovenous fistulas, the balloon catheter is detached and the subject is suffering from paraplegia of the lower limbs. The permanent disability has been assessed at 60%. The decision of the 'Conseil d'Etat' says:[107]

> Whereas if the act intended, even completed within the state of the art, exposes to known risks of death or disability, the patient should be informed, under conditions that allow to collect informed consent. If this information is not required in an emergency, inability or refusal of the patient to be informed, the mere fact that the risks are realized only in exceptional circumstances does not exempt practitioners of their obligation to inform the individual of risk of paraplegia that involved the intervention.

III. The Causal Link Between the Lack of Information and the Damage

218. In front of the civil and administrative jurisdictions, to ensure that liability is qualified, it is necessary to make evidence that the lack of information is at the origin of damage. But the damage is not linked with the lack of information, but to the possible side effect of the medical act. Some jurisdictions indemnify only a lack of chance to avoid the damage.

Nevertheless, the argument usually developed by patients or by their counsellors is that if the subject was informed of the risks, it would not have consented. So the act

104. Bruchet CE 31 janvier 1964 Lebon p. 71.
105. voir AM DUGUET La faute médicale à l'hôpital Editions Berger Levrault deuxième édition p. 140.
106. For example the closure by surgery, with extracorporeal circulation of a ventricular septal defect is a procedure such that, given the nature of the condition being treated, the failure to inform the patient of the risks cannot be a fault CE 6 Jul. 1984 Puccio RDSS 1985 p. 49.
107. Voir C Esper L'information médicale du malade à l'hôpital public. Gaz Pal 17 19 dec. 2000.

would not have been performed, thus avoiding the risk exposure. Some jurisdictions compensated for this reason the entire damage estimating that it would not have realized if the informed patient has chosen not to comply.

Thus it is necessary that the patient has a real choice to refuse to act, which is not the case when the medical act is indispensable. In those circumstances, despite information on the risk, the patient would have accepted the medical act. Then the lack of information has not deprived the patient of exposure to risk which would have realized anyway.

This solution was chosen by the Court of Appeal of Angers[108] after cassation of the Judgment of 25 February 1997 which says that:

> even informed the patient would have consented to the act because the intervention was necessary and without it, the patient's condition would have been worse than the condition in which he was after the occurrence of the unrevealed risk. So the practitioner did not commit any fault which contributed to the realization of this risk.

This position was confirmed by the Cour dė Cassation,[109] in these terms:

> the decision noted that Mr. H, whose father died of a colon cancer, wanted to get rid of painful intestinal problems and fears for the future…he was suffering ulcerative disease facilitating the occurrence of cancer… the polyps found should be removed because of the risk of degeneration into cancer. With a sovereign appreciation from these findings the Court of Appeal states that, only informed of the risk of perforation, Mr H would refuse nor the examination nor the removal of the polyp so that there was no justification for any compensable injury.

108. CA Angers 11 septembre 1998. Médecine et droit, n° 33, 1998, page 27.
109. 20 Jun. 2000 (Civ. Bulletin No. 193).

Chapter 3. The Respect of Patients' Rights in Medical Practice

§1. The Modalities of the Information: Oral Information or a Written Document?

219. Following the decision of 27 February 1997, scientific societies have come together to develop materials to provide information to the patients. Writing those documents has sometimes been difficult since the information has to be raised so as not to frighten the patient. The scientific quality of information must comply with the current state of medical knowledge, hence the need for consensus among professionals. The consensus serves also as a reference for the experts in courts.

Each professional is the sole judge of how he or she would like to inform patients. The physician informs consciousness according to the potentiality of the risk occurrence and its severity. The written document, if any, does not exempt the detailed oral information on the specific consequences of the act to each patient. The physician should ensure that the information has been understood.

I. Written Consents

220. A written informed consent is necessary in specific medical activities, which are regulated in the Public Health Code.

For *medical research*, the Article L 1122-1-1 requires a free and an informed consent given after a specific information defined by the Article L 1122-1 CSP. The consent is written or in case of impossibility certified by third person independent from the sponsor or the investigator.

In case of *medical assisted procreation*, the consent (Article L 2141-10) is expressed by the two members of the couple after a specific information delivered by a multidisciplinary team. After a one-month period for reflection, the confirmation of consent is asked in written. When gametes from donor are to be used, the consent is given in front of the civil judge or the notary (Articles 319 and 320 of the Civil Code). In that case, the aim of the information is to tell the couple of the consequences on filiation of the gamete donation which forbids any paternity contest.

To analyse *the genetic characteristics* of a patient, the French law is very protective: the free and informed consent is given in writing (Article L 1131-1 CSP) after a specific information delivered by a genetic counselling committee in the conditions of the Article R 1131-5 CSP. When the analysis is prescribed on a minor, the potential results should bring preventive or curatives measures; if they do not, the analysis must not be performed.

The pregnant women must consent in writing to cytogenetic and biological analysis for *prenatal diagnosis* after she has been informed by a genetic counselling committee of the risks for the child to be born to present a very serious disease, of the characteristics of the disease, the possible treatment, and the results the prenatal diagnosis can bring. The frame of the document of information is defined by a decree. A copy of the consent form is filed by the establishment performing the analysis (Article R 2131-7 CSP).

The organ *donation by a living donor* can be performed after the consent in front of the civil judge. The potential donor is informed by a committee of experts (Article L 1231-3 CSP) of the risks and the consequences of the organ donation, and the judge will control that the potential donor has correctly understood the risks.

§2. The Information Content

221. In the medical team, if several practitioners are treating the same patient, each physician is responsible for his information, and shall provide the information according to his competence, if necessary in conjunction with his colleagues. In accordance with Article 64 of the Code of Medical Ethics which states: '*When several physicians collaborate in the examination or in the treatment of a patient, they must keep each other informed. Each practitioner assumes personal responsibility and ensures the patient's information.*'

Scientific societies believe that the information relates to: the definition of treatment or technique to be applied, the description of various steps in the treatment, the type of anaesthesia if any, the duration of hospitalization, the complications, and possible disadvantages described by the medical art. On the occurrence of a complication, it is necessary to explain how to fix it.

The information also covers the foreseeable consequences with a special attention regarding the scars, the long-term side effects, the precautions, if any, the patient has to respect and more generally all the information needed to manage his or her health.

§3. Information about the Serious Risks and the Risk-Benefit Balance

222. The predictable risks created by the therapeutic act should be proportioned to the benefit. The therapeutic benefit justifies, in many cases, invasive or mutilating treatments. Some so-called comfort anaesthesia performed at the request of the subject, may constitute a risk of complication. It is up to physician to ensure that the precautions be redoubled. For such non-therapeutic acts, it is important that the subject has understood what dangers he or she exposes himself, and the surgical team should not carry anything that could entail an undue risk to the patient.[110]

When the risks of an innovative surgery have not already been identified such as laser thermotherapy, the argument saying that as the risks are not known the doctor is allowed to certify that the surgery has no risks at all is not acceptable. The Conseil

110. Article 40 du code de déontologie médicale.

d'Etat considers that the lack of information on the risks constitutes a fault and opens the way to indemnification.[111]

For a long time, the obligation of information in cosmetic surgery has always been considered by the civil jurisprudence as a reinforced obligation on all possible risks, including the scars. In addition, since 2002[112] the consent to cosmetic surgery is collected after delivery of an estimate. Approaching the consumers' rights, this requirement reflects the desire to have a better participation of the patient in the decision-making, thereby changing the doctor-patient relationship. The Article L 6322-2 CSP states that the information must present the conditions of the surgery, the potential risks and side effects, then leave a period of reflection (without any time limit), before the expression of consent. The law does not impose a written consent, though the cosmetic surgeons do.

To perform cosmetic surgery, an authorization is required after an accreditation procedure (Article L 6322-1 CSP). In addition, the National Council of the College of Physicians by making publicly available information relating to the qualification of professionals practising cosmetic surgery,[113] contributes to a better patients' information.

The obligation to provide information does not end when the patient has consented to the act. It must include information on the suites and provide details on the scars or possible sequellae, '*throughout the disease, the physician considers the patient's personality in the explanations and ensure their understanding*' (Article 35 of the Code of Medical Ethics).

§4. Traceability of the Information

223. According to his specialty, the physician will choose the most appropriate mean: he or she may note in the medical record the information provided to the patient, with the date, the circumstances, and the content of the information. This may be supplemented by a letter to the family doctor informing him of the risks of the examination and certifying that the patient has been informed. The physician may also invite his colleague to renew the information to the patient.

For procedures requiring a particularly difficult choice, the information should be renewed, and if necessary the patient is requested to be accompanied by a person of his entourage.

The 2002 law on patient's rights provides a special disposition for the official designation of a trustworthy person in the Article L 1111-6 CSP:

> Any adult may designate a trustworthy person who can be a parent, a relative or a general practitioner who will be consulted when the patient becomes unable to express his or her wishes and to receive the necessary information for that purpose. This designation shall be in writing. It is revocable at any time. If the

111. CE, 10 Mai, 2017 : n° 397840 . Revue droit et santé n°79 p. 722.
112. Article 52,1 de la loi 2002-303.
113. Website of national College of Physicians CNOM: www.ordmed.org.

patient wishes, the trustworthy person accompanying him on his actions and attend medical appointments to help in decisions.

Apart from the cases prescribed by law such as termination of pregnancy, biomedical research, assisted reproduction, medical act performed on a prisoner out of an emergency, asking the patient to sign documents for bringing information may seem excessive.

I. Should the Physician Give the Whole Information?

224. The Code of Medical Ethics, in Article 35 provides that for legitimate reasons that the physician appreciates in conscience, a patient may be left in ignorance of a severe diagnosis or prognosis. Too wide information may traumatize patients and dissuade him or her from accepting hazardous but necessary treatment for him. This traditional position of physicians[114] is widely criticized in public as medical paternalism. But the 'Cour de Cassation'[115] has approved the therapeutic limitations of the information, when it appears to the physician that the risk information is likely to have a negative influence on the necessity of investigation or care.[116]

II. Does the Physician Have the Obligation to Convince the Patient?

225. Generally, when the patient does not consent, the physician tries to explain the consequences of the refusal to make him or her change the decision.

The Article 11 of the law on patient rights[117] considers the patient as a partner in the decision-making, by saying that:

> any person takes with the health professional, in the light of information provided, decisions regarding the health. The physician should respect the will of the person who has been informed of the consequences of his or her personal choice. If the will of the person to refuse or withdraw 'all' treatment is life-threatening, the physician should do everything possible to make the patient accept essential treatment. He can call for advice another member of the medical profession. In all cases the patient has to reiterate the request within a reasonable time.

---

114. L René ' De l'information au consentement éclairé 'Bull de l'ordre des médecins nov 1989.
115. Cass Civ 23 mai 2000 Semaine Juridique 10 342.
116. voir G Memeteau Cours de droit médical Les Etudes Hospitalières p. 275.
117. Article L 1111-4 CSP.

Chapter 4. Professional Secrecy

226. Respect of the professional secrecy for the doctors and the healthcare professionals, is a deontological and legal obligation. The deontological foundation goes back up to the Hippocratic oath which imposes on the doctor to say nothing about what he would have heard or understood when he enters into his patient's house while the Penal Code punishes the offence established by the disclosure of a secret by his possessor.

§1. Definitions and General Principle

I. Private Life, Confidentiality and Professional Secrecy

227. French law protects the right to private life in Article 9 of the Civil Code: 'Everyone has the right to respect for his private life.' Private life is a subjective human right that must be respected by all. Criminal sanctions are provided for violation of someone's private life (Article 226-1) that applies to all citizens. Courts now compensate for consequences of such violation. The jurisprudence of civil courts has defined private life as covering everything related to the person, his family, his home and his health. Only the individual himself or their beneficiaries may authorize the disclosure of his private life.

Confidentiality is the respect for the confidential nature of an information by the person who is depository when this information is either given directly by the person himself or herself or when any other person who is led to know it, through the documents to which he or she could access (correspondence, records, reports). The obligation of confidentiality is imposed on all professionals who are thereby led to know the elements of privacy and all information relating to the person and his or her family. The obligation of confidentiality is associated with the civil servants status.

More broadly, all secret information brought to the attention of professionals is protected, and the disclosure is punished under the Penal Code by section 226-13: '*The disclosure of a secret information by a person who is the possessor/depository either by his status or his profession or due to a function or to a temporary assignment is punished with imprisonment of one year and a fine of € 15,000.*'

Concerning doctors and health professionals the various codes of conduct/ deontology or rules for professionals recall their duties to respect professional secrecy in accordance with the law. Thus, professionals who disclose secret information expose themselves to both penal and disciplinary sanctions.

II. A Professional Secrecy General and Absolute

228. The sanction for a violation of professional secrecy is a punishable offence since the first publication of Penal Code. The original Article 378 of the Penal Code was addressed to doctors, surgeons, and any person holding confidences that he or she received during his or her practice.

The obligation to respect the professional secrecy is of public policy, which means that every citizen must be sure to confide to any professional doctor, lawyer, solicitor or priest, without being afraid that their secrets could be revealed.

In 1885, the French Supreme Criminal Court in the case *Watelet*[118] pronounced a penal sanction. It is the decision held in principle on the professional secrecy of doctors. Since then, the relationship between doctor and patient, and the need to transmit information without the presence or consent of the person concerned has led the legislator to permit exceptions from the principle. However, the general principle remains, and it was reaffirmed in 1996 and 1999 in the case of the book: 'Le grand secret' in which the doctor of the President of the Republic has published revelations about the state of health of his patient. He was criminally punished, removed from the College of Physicians, and the book was banned from publication,[119] even if it had been available on the Internet.

The deontological basis of the professional secrecy: Article 4 (Article R 4127-4 CSP) states the obligation to respect professional secrecy in accordance with the law and defines the content,[120] that is to say, not only the confidence, but also everything the doctor has seen, heard or understood when practising.

Moreover medical ethics requires compliance by the secret to people attending physicians (R 4127-72)[121] and ensures the protection of medical documents and correspondence (Article R 4127-73 CSP).

§2. Breach of Privacy

229. Breach of privacy is achieved by the interference of third parties in the private sphere without permission of the subject. This interference is sanctioned by civil courts for any damage and disturbance and the courts can stop the infringement by the seizure of books or of newspapers. There is a special disciplinary sanction for the doctor in accordance with Article 51 of the Code of Medical Ethics '*the doctor shall not interfere without any professional reason in the family affairs or in the privacy of patients*'.

118. Cour de Cassation 19 décembre 1885.
119. The book written by Claude Gubler and Michel Gonod published by Plon in 1996 has been forbidden by justice. 40,000 issues have been sold before the interdiction. After the decision of the European Court of Human Rights based on freedom of expression, the book is published since 2005 . 'Le grand secret' à nouveau en librairie 18 Février 2005. www.yempsreel.novelobs.com visited on 17 Dec. 2017.
120. Professional secrecy established in the interest of patients applies to any doctor in the terms established by law. The secret covers everything came to the knowledge of the physician in the practise of his profession, that is to say not only what has been entrusted to him, but what he saw, heard or understood.
121. The physician must ensure that the people who assist him in the exercise should be educated about their obligations of professional secrecy and comply. It should ensure that no harm is carried by his entourage to secrecy that attaches to his professional correspondence.

§3. The Professional Secrecy Protected by the Penal Code

230. Respecting the secret is a guarantee for one who confides in somebody. Article 226-13 of the Penal Code says 'The disclosure of secret information *by a person who is the possessor/depository either by his state or his profession or due to a function or to a temporary assignment*, is punished with imprisonment of one year and a fine of € 15,000.'

I. Exemptions: Authorization to Disclose to a Designated Third Party

231. An exemption is a permission to disclose secret information without incurring sanctions. The exemption defines a strict framework for disclosure and refers to the persons to whom it is possible to transmit the secret information. Exceptions are provided by the Penal Code and various laws and regulations.

Exemptions thus defined are authorizations permitting the information to be exchanged between professionals and some institutions and to facilitate access to social benefits.

However, the obligation to disclose is imposed by the Penal Code which sanctions the failure to report for example deprivation, physical abuse, and sexual violence against a person who had knowledge of such acts. Contrary to what one might think, there are very few situations that require a doctor to disclose the facts which he had known of during his practice, and the courts have clearly ruled some situations, allowing in many circumstances the doctor to remain silent.

The constrained disclosure is sometimes felt by health professionals as an act of betrayal, and doctors hide behind their obligation to professional secrecy, not to deliberately conceal the information to third parties who claim to know it, but to meet the commitment of their oath.

II. The Exemptions in the Penal Code

232. Article 226–14 of the Penal Code authorizes disclosure in very specific situations: for any professional who informs legal, medical or administrative authorities of deprivation or physical abuse, including sexual abuse or mutilation that he was aware of and that have been inflicted on a minor or a person who is not able to protect herself.[122]

For the doctor who, with the consent of the victim, informs the Public Prosecutor of abuse or physical or psychic deprivation that he noticed in the practise of his profession and allow him to assume that physical, sexual or psychological violence were committed. The consent of the victim is not necessary if it is a minor or a person unable to protect herself.

122. The Law of 5 Mar. 2007a made an exception to the principle of consent of the victim, provided that it is not able to protect themselves because of age or physical or mental condition.

For health professionals or of social protection services who inform the 'préfet' (representative of the State at the local level) about the dangerousness of the person who consult them and about whom they know they own a gun or have expressed their intention to acquire one.

The report to the competent authorities made in accordance with Article 226-14 cannot be punished by disciplinary sanctions. But only exemptions expressly provided for in Article 226-14 of the Penal Code are possible under the strict interpretation of criminal law.[123]

III. Other Exemptions

233. These are authorizations to disclose secret information to designated third parties. This is the case of certain medical certificates: for birth, death, accidents at work and occupational diseases, reporting of pregnancy, etc.

Further exemptions fall within the field of public health or of public order: statement of contagious and venereal diseases, reporting of dangerous alcoholics, for hospitalization of the mentally ill; certificates given to the judge to request a guardianship to a person incapable of protecting himself or herself. The legal protection measures are: 'tutelle' (guardianship), 'curatelle' (curatorship), 'sauvegarde de justice'.[124]

§4. The Obligation to Report a Physical Abuse or a Sexual Abuse

234. The legal obligation to report is imposed on all citizens (Article 434-1 of the Penal Code)[125] but excludes persons subject to professional secrecy. The report is an authorization for professionals compelled to secrecy and not an obligation. Article 44[126] of the Code of Medical Ethics considers the doctor as the protector of the victim.

---

123. Article and CP 111-4 in the situations referred to in Art. 223-6 CP (failure to rescue … denunciation of HIV.

124. 'sauvegarde de justice' is a temporary measure of protection when the person is unable to express his or her will due to a disease.

125. Article CP 434-1 'The fact that anyone with knowledge of deprivation, abuse or sexual abuse inflicted on a minor under fifteen years of age or a person who is not able to protect herself or himself because of its age, illness, infirmity, physical or mental disability or pregnancy, not to inform the judicial or administrative authorities is punishable by three years imprisonment and EUR 45,000 fine.' When a doctor discerns a person from whom it is called is a victim of abuse or deprivation he or she must implement the most appropriate means to protect the person, with caution and circumspection. When there is a child under 15 or a person who is not able to protect herself or himself because of physical or mental condition, the physician must, except in special circumstances that he or she appreciates in conscience, alert medical administrative judicial authorities.

126. Article R4127-44 CSP When a physician discerns a person is a victim of abuse or deprivation he must implement the most appropriate means to protect he or she, acting with caution and circumspection. In the case of minors or persons who are not able to protect themselves, because of age or physical or mental condition, the physician alerts the judicial or administrative authorities, except in special circumstances that he or she appreciates in conscience.

§5. The Legislation of 4 March 2002 the Article 1110-4

235. In this Article, the legislator takes up the main ethical obligations of professional secrecy and its applications in the performance of activities of care and protection by the health professionals and institutions. It enshrines the right to respect private life and confidentiality of information concerning any person that a professional or an institution takes into care.

The secret's content covers all information about the person who came to the knowledge of health professionals and all staff member. It applies to all health professionals and all professionals involved in the health system. Unless the person explicitly refuses it, the transmission of information among professionals is possible to ensure continuity of care or to ensure the best healthcare services. When a person's care is covered by a team of health professionals in a health facility, the information about this person are deemed to be given by the patient to the entire team.

236. Safeguards to protect the confidentiality of data are organized in accordance with the recommendations of the 'Commission Nationale informatique et Libertés' CNIL.[127] A new offence is punishable: obtaining or attempting to obtain copies of this information in violation of this section is punishable with imprisonment of one year and EUR 15,000 fine.

Towards third parties, medical confidentiality does not preclude the family, relatives of the sick person or the person of trust defined in Article L 1111-6 receive the necessary information to enable them to provide direct support to it, unless opposed him.

Finally professional secrecy does not prevent information about a deceased person from being delivered to its rightful owners, unless a contrary intention by the person before his death has been notified.

§6. The Protection of Secret Information

I. The Patient

237. The patient himself cannot see the object privilege to have access to information about it. However, Article 35 of the Code of Ethics and Article L 1110-4 provides that the doctor can be silent on the grave prognosis and the doctor then informs the relatives. Thus, the doctor must inform the patient of a graver prognosis in situations where the disease exposes others to a risk of contamination.

II. The Spouse

238. The doctor has no right to disclose findings or diagnosis; this information remains secret. The patient has a broad right of direct access to personal information (Article L 1112-2 CSP). The patient's wills prevail in the transmission of information

127. National commission for data protection www.cnil.fr.

about it. Regarding health insurance, the patient is deemed to have given his consent to the transmission of information (agreement in the Convention).

The patient is free to disclose any medical information about him. However it can neither allow the physician to disclose, nor to testify in court.

III. The Family

239. The family is considered as a third party, except in accordance with Article 35. However, Article L 1111-7 CSP, which gives patients access to their information, provides that in case of death, the access by rights holders is possible under the conditions defined by Article L 1110-4 within eight days to know the causes of death.

IV. The Minor

240. The doctor is bound by the obligation of confidentiality towards the minor. He cannot inform parents or guardians if the minor refuses it. Article L 111-5 of the CSP in derogation of Article 372-1 of the Civil Code[128] provides that the doctor can refrain himself from getting the consent of the holder of parental authority before taking medical decisions when the treatment or intervention is necessary to save the health of a minor, if he or she expressly objects to the consultation of the holder of parental authority.[129]

A minor who wishes to keep secret a treatment or an intervention that he or she has underwent may refuse the doctor to communicate to the holders of parental authority information related to these medical procedures.[130]

V. Other Doctors and Physicians Providing Control Activities

241. Apart from exchanges between professionals in the interest of the patient and for the organization of continuity of care, confidentiality even exists between doctors. A doctor cannot take advantage of his professional title as a doctor to access a patient's record to which he does not give any treatment.

Thus, a medical officer of a private insurance company is guilty of the offence of breach of professional secrecy for disclosing to his company any medical information that were taken from the medical record of a patient who received a treatment at the hospital.[131]

128. Act n° 2002-305 du 4 mars 2002 relative à l'autorité parentale JORF 5 mars 2002.
129. See CE 17,November 2006, n° 270863, Juridata n° 2006-071118.
130. Décret 2002-637 du 29 avril 2002 on acces to personal data stored by health professionnals and the healthcare facilities Art. 6. On the emergence of autonomous rights of the Minor M Penneau, Le droit au secret des informations dans la loi du 4 mars 2002 in La Loi du 4 mars 2002: continuité ou nouveauté en droit médical PUF 2003, p. 101.
131. Cass crim 1973,n° 72-91.592.

The insurance consultant cannot produce a document covered by medical secrecy unless the assured has renounced to the benefit of secrecy and that the judge, in case of difficulty and, if necessary after an investigative measure, assesses whether the opposition of subject tends to enforce a legitimate interest.[132]

242. The insurance company cannot require direct access to the medical file. The court refused the direct transmission to the company.[133] As the doctor can give his patient any medical document that may concern him or her, he cannot directly transmit the information to the doctor of the insurance company.

In accordance with the ethical principles,[134] the documents submitted by the subject himself to the doctor appointed by the insurance company, cannot be directly communicated to the insurance company, only a technical notice is given to the company.

The insurance medical doctors acting as consultants from the national state health insurance office have a status which confers them a total independence towards the administrative services of the insurance office in order to respect the secrecy of information they collect from the policyholders.

Article L 161-36-1 from the Code of Social Security has created a personal health record (DMP) to promote coordination, quality, and continuity of care. The DMP is made from all the data mentioned in Article L 1111-8 CSP in respect of medical secrecy. Each act performed by a health professional is mentioned in the DMP, and the professional states whether the patient has authorized the DMP consultation before performing the act.

Article 3 of the Act of 13 August 2004[135] states that access to the personal health record may not be required out of the provisions of the Article L 161-36-2 of the Code of the SS, even with the consent of the person concerned. Access to the personal health record is prohibited at the conclusion of a contract for additional protection, or any other contract requiring the assessment of health status.

The personal health record cannot be required neither for the conclusion of any contract nor during its performance. It cannot be accessed by the occupational medicine services. Any failure results in the application of the penalties provided for in Article 226-13 of the CP.

VI. The Employer

243. The doctor cannot directly transmit confidential information to the employer. As for the medical examinations related to a job application or to the surveillance of employees, the occupational doctor will only send to the employer an administrative notice of ability to the job.

For accidents at work and occupational disease, there is a special exemption that allows to mention medical information on the certificate provided to the health insurance

132. Cass civ, 2 juin 2005, n° 04-13.509.
133. Cass 2 ième Civ 2 Juin 2005 n° 04-13.862.
134. Robert Saury Rapport Secret médical et compagnies d'assurances Conseil national de l'Ordre des médecins, Avril 2000.
135. Loi n° 2004-810 du 13 août 2004 relative à la réforme de l'assurance maladie.

and that entitles to social benefits. An employer who wishes to challenge the professional nature of the accident or illness has to do directly with the social security office.

VII. The Police and Judicial Authorities

244. Situations allowing police or justice to access to medical information covered by professional secrecy are very strictly defined by the Code of Penal Procedure.

A doctor may be required by order of the law to undertake a medical examination, but cannot be required to provide the information he learned in the exercise of his functions.

Thus, report to the police authorities of patients suffering from gunshot wounds is not compulsory, and the professional who would make such a declaration is exposed to criminal sanctions.

Concerning drugs addictions, the principle is first to consider the addict as a person requiring health care and not as a criminal. Addicts who have to treat their addiction in hospitals may request anonymity (Article L 3414-1 CSP). Moreover, illegal narcotics introduced by patients in a health facility must be given to the competent authorities without disclosing the identity of the patient.[136]

VIII. The Medical Doctor's Testimony in Court

245. In courts, the doctor is allowed to violate professional secrecy, to give the evidence of his good faith or competence to the judges; this disclosure is limited to the strict requirements of its defence.[137]

Facts were different in the case decided by the Court of Appeal of Aix where the doctor used documents from a patient's personal medical record who was treated in the institution where he was working to establish the falsity of a certificate used in court against him.[138]

---

136. Instruction du 13 avril 2011.
137. TGI Paris 26 juin 1998 BICC, 1998, n° 1390. Droits de la défense (voir doc n° 13).
138. *Aix en Provence 27 février 2008 Juris-data n° 2008-362577.*

Chapter 5. Specific Activities

§1. Organ Transplantation and Procurement

246. Since 1976, the French legislator has organized donation and transplantation of organs. By this time, the organ donation by brain dead subjects prevailed. The so-called Caillavet[139] Act provides that organs can be harvested from the body of a deceased person who did not mention during her lifetime her refusal to such a donation. The presumption of consent has been maintained in successive legislation as well as for the principles of anonymity and free, which already existed for blood donation.

On the non-commercialization of the human body, the National Consultative Advisory Committee on ethics[140] said:

> A kidney cannot be sold by the one where it came from, or be sold by a third party regardless of incentives intended person who receives it. Such incentives could generate up to blackmail on detainees or on any dominated minority. Human dignity is at stake if financial gain becomes the result of physical weakness, even temporary.

In 1994, for the first time, the legislator imposed respect of the integrity of the human body.[141] Previously, only the rights of the individual were protected in the Civil Code. The law ignored the human body in itself.

In terms of principles, the 94-653 Act in respect of the human body is innovative because it focuses not only on the human body but more broadly on the individual and the species. It prohibits surrogacy. The act introduces a section 16 of the Civil Code which recognizes the primacy of the individual, prohibits any violation to his dignity and guarantees respect for the human being from the beginning of his life. Inviolability and non-commercialization of the body are enshrined in Article 16-1.

Breach of the integrity of the human species is prohibited (Article 16-4) and any eugenic practice aimed at organizing the selection of persons. Criminal penalty is prescribed for any deviation to of practices.

A major provision about consent will change medical practices because now the attempt to integrity of the human body can be undermined only in case of medical necessity for the person or exceptionally in the therapeutic interest of another person,[142] and the interested person's consent must be obtained in advance, except in cases where his state required a therapeutic intervention in which he is not able to consent.

139. Act 76-1181 of 22 Dec. 1976.
140. Opinion n° 21 CCNE 13/12/90.www.ccne-ethique.fr.
141. 29 Jul. 1994 94-653 Act on respect for the human body and the 94-654 act on the donation and use of elements and products of the human body to medical assistance, procreation and prenatal diagnosis.
142. Article 16-3 of the Civil Code.

These temporary laws have been updated by the 2004-800 Act on bioethics which, due to the shortage of organs, expanded the scope of potential donors to living persons and authorized the removal of organs on non-hart beating persons in 2011.

I. Purpose and General Principles

247. The procurement and use of elements and products of the human body, including their import and export, should have a medical or scientific purpose or be conducted on request of the justice in legal proceedings (Article L 1211-1 CSP).

No payment, regardless of form, may be allocated to persons consenting to the removal of parts of their body or to the collection of their human products. (Article L 1211-4).

The donor may not know the identity of the recipient, and the recipient the identity of the donor. No information identifying the donor or the recipient may be disclosed. (Article L 1211-5). There can be exception to this principle of anonymity only in cases of medical necessity.

A risk-benefit balance should be evaluated for the recipient, and the rules of safety compliance shall be respected. (Article L 1211-6).

II. Conditions for Removal

248. The removal from a living person is organized by Article L 1231-1 CSP. It is exclusively for the therapeutic benefit of the recipient. The donor is the father or mother of the recipient. By way of derogation it may be the spouse, brother or sister, son or daughter, grandparents, uncle, cousin, spouse of the father or of the mother, the person who has evidence of a common life with the recipient for two years.

The information is given by an expert committee composed of five members. The consent is given in front of the President of the TGI or in an emergency in front of the Public Prosecutor. The consent may be revoked at any time.

The removal from a living minor or from an adult protected by the law is prohibited (except for bone marrow transplantation).

III. Removal from a Deceased Person (1232-1 CSP)

249. Removal is made in the therapeutic interest of the recipient or for a scientific purpose in the context of a research protocol, from a person who did not express her or his refusal during the lifetime. Refusal is expressed by any means (including a computerized national registry). Relatives are informed about the removal. On this occasion, they can give to removal team information about the patient's wishes that they may have collected during lifetime.

The removal from a deceased minor or from an adult protected by the law cannot be done without the consent of the both parents or the guardians.

IV. Consent to Removal of Organs

250. The removal of parts of the human body and the collection of its products cannot be practised without the prior consent of the donor. This consent may be revoked at any time. (Article L 1211-2).

The provisions relating to removal of organs from a living subject: 'no organ removal for donation can be carried out on a living minor person or on a living person subject to a measure of legal protection'.

By way of derogation, a bone marrow sample can be performed on a minor for the benefit of his brother or sister.

This removal can only be realized with the consent of each holder of parental authority or legal guardian of the minor. The consent is expressed in front of the President of the High Court or the judge appointed by him. In case of an emergency, the consent is collected by any means by the Public Prosecutor.

Authorization for the removal is granted by a committee of experts which ensures that the minor was informed about the removal to express his or her will if he or she has the capacity to understand. The refusal of the minor must be respected and hinders the removal.

V. The Expression of Refusal

251. Refusal can be expressed by any means, including enrolment in a national computerized registry (Article L 1232-1). The functioning of the registry is defined in Articles 5-14 R 61232-CSP. It is placed under the control of the ABM. The refusal is revocable at any time. *In 2016,* the law of Modernization of the Health System[143] plans to improve the information of the users and to associate more the latter with the health policy. The Decree 2016-1118 of August 11, 2016[144] relating to the expression of the refusal of organ harvesting after the death allows to take into account, the oral expression of the refusal in front of the family since the subject during his lifetime was not registered on the refusal register. Thus, the decree provides three types of expression of the refusal, (a) the registration on the National Automated Register, (b) any document expressing the refusal in writing dated and signed by its author and entrusted to a relative , and (c) the refusal expressed in front of a relative. The refusal is transcribed '*in writing mentioning the context and the circumstances of its expression, dated and signed by the relative who makes the claim and by the team of hospital coordination*' (Article R 1232-4-4 III).

If the deceased person is a minor or an adult under a measure of legal protection, the removal for a transplant can be carried out only if each holder of the parental authority or the legal representative expressly consents in writing.

Concerning organ removal for research or scientific purposes other than those aiming at investigating the causes of death, the removal cannot be made without the consent of the deceased, expressed directly or by the testimony of his or her family. However, when the deceased is a minor, consent is given by one of the holders of

143. Article 192 Loi 2016-41 du 26 Janvier 2016 JO du 14 Août 2016 www.legifrance.gouv.fr.
144. JO n° 0189 du 14 août 2016 In force since 1 Jan. 2017.

parental authority. The family is informed of the samples removed to investigate the cause of death.

VI. The Diagnosis of Brain Death

252. Doctors who establish the death of brain on the one hand, and those who carry out the removal or transplantation on the other, must be part of separate services.

Removals may only be carried out if the person is brain-dead, whose signs are described in a decree. For a person under mechanical ventilation and maintaining a hemodynamic function, the certificate of brain death must be signed by two doctors and mention the results of the EEG or angiography.

Doctors retain a copy of the certificate; a copy is given to the director of the establishment where the removals are made, and the original is kept in the medical record of the deceased.

Since 2005, there is a possibility of removals on non-heart beating persons. It is stated in the Article R -1232-4-1 that removals of organs, whose list is fixed by decree, can be practised on a dead person with a cardiac and respiratory persistent arrest.

After removals, by respect of the dignity of the donor, the reconstruction of the body is mandatory. (Article L 1232-5 CSP)

VII. Tissue Samples and Cells

253. For the harvesting of hematopoietic cells in the bone marrow, the terms for obtaining the consent are similar to those of the removal of organs. The consent is given in writing in front of the President of High Court, or in an emergency, in front of the Public Prosecutor. (The Article 1241-1).

For minors, the scope of donors is extended for the benefit of his brother or sister exceptionally his cousin, uncle, aunt, nephew, and niece. An expert committee will ensure that everything has been done to find a donor, and that the minor has been informed. The refusal of the minor forbids the removal (Article 1241-3). As for protected adults, terms are similar (Article 1241-4).

VIII. Transplants Review

254. The 2016 activity report of the ABM[145] shows that the activity exceeded the objective of the annual plan with 2.5% more transplants (5891 in 2016 against 5746 in 2015). The number of transplants performed under the Maastricht III programme (sampling of subjects in the context of a withdrawal of treatment) increased with 114 transplants in 2016, as well as live donor transplants (576) representing 16% of renal transplants. Since January 2016, a centralized living donor secretariat has been set up.

145. www.agence-biomedecine.fr.

333 living donors were auditioned during the 124 sessions organized by the agency. Despite these efforts, 22,617 patients are on the waiting list.

Among 3676 persons with brain death in 2016, only 1770 5 have been involved in transplantation process. The lack of harvesting is the consequence of the opposition expressed by the person during his or her life time: 37.1%, and by the family 60.8 (1.2% more than in 2015), and the pathologies of potential donor which are not compatible with transplantation (0.4%). The emotional factor prevails over with a hierarchy of organs especially for corneas because the eye is very strongly symbolic. In France, the presumed consent of the donor allows removing organs without asking the family, but the transplantation team considers 'unacceptable to override the expressed opposition of the family'.

Due to the shortage of grafts, the promotion and development of transplantation are considered as a national priority governed by the principle of equity in the allocation of grafts (Article L 1231-1).

However, advertising for a donation of elements or products of the human body for the benefits of a particular person or for an institution or specified body is prohibited. This prohibition does not preclude the public information for the donation of elements and products of the human body (Article L 1211-3). Promotional campaigns on organ donation have started in 1998 organized by the Agency of Biomedicine. Since 2000, a National Day of Reflection on Organ Donation and Donor Recognition has been held on June 22. A major communication campaign on the refusal mechanism was organized at the end of 2016 and was widely covered by the media.[146]

Physicians ensure that their patients from 16 to 25 years old are informed of the terms of consent to organ donation for transplantation purpose and, failing that, deliver this information to them individually as soon as possible. (Article L 1211-3).

§2. Medically Assisted Procreation

I. A Gradual Legal and Regulatory Construction Preceded by an Ethical Reflection

255. Once conservation of the human sperm became possible and proposed techniques of artificial procreation, professionals started being concerned about the consequences of these new methods. The ethical reflection conducted by academic fertility centres (CECOS) and centres for assisted reproduction has been the source of 94-654 Act on donation and use of human body, the assisted procreation, and prenatal diagnosis. Confronted with the development of new methods, the temporary law was revised in 2004 (2004-800 bioethics law) and the latest version dates from 2011 (2011-814 Act of 7 July 2011).

These new technologies have had an impact on the law of filiations. Once a couple accepted this method because of the couple's infertility, usually related to the sterility of the husband, the latter had the right to refuse, in case of a divorce to contribute

146. Agence de la Biomédecine 2016 report, p. 40.

to the cost of education of a child; he could easily deny paternity because of his inability to procreate.

256. The Civil Code has taken into account this new situation, in the interest of the child. Article 311-20 provides that the consent given to the MAP before a notary or judge prohibits any action to establish or contest filiations. Whoever, having consented to the MAP does not recognize the child shall be liable to the mother or child.

In French law, as surrogacy is prohibited,[147] there cannot be any contested maternity, the mother being legally considered as the woman who gives birth to the child.

To the fundamental principles of no paid and anonymous donation, were added very strict conditions for the couple applying to the MAP which remained unchanged since 1994 namely a couple made of a man and a woman of childbearing age who form a parental project.

257. While our European neighbours grant MAP more broadly: singles, couples of the same-sex, regardless of age … and despite the development of a reproductive tourism at a global scale, the French legislator has not provided any flexibility in the 2011 revision. The National Ethics Advisory Committee has maintained its original principles while some of its members were in favour of flexibility in certain circumstances including surrogacy.

However in the context of the law allowing the same-sex marriage adopted by the Parliament,[148] there still might be some adjustments to be made to the French legislation.

Another revision of the bioethics law is in preparation for 2018 and the CCNE (National Ethics Advisory Committee) wants to associate the citizens to this reflection.[149] Regarding the techniques of medical assistance to procreation, the CCNE said that these techniques originally authorized by law to address the infertility of the couple, are sought today to meet societal demands that go beyond the current framework provided by law. The committee explored three situations: oocyte self-preservation in young women, requests for donor insemination by couples of women and single women, and applications for surrogacy[150]

II. The Current Legal Framework

A. Definition

258. MAP refers to clinical and biological practices for in vitro design, conservation of gametes, germinal tissue and embryos, embryo transfer, and artificial insemination. (Article L 2141-1 CSP).

147. Article 16-7 of the Civil Code: A convention on surrogacy is void.
148. Law 2013-404, 17 Mai 2013 Opening marriage to same sex couples.
149. http://up-magazine.info/index.php/bio-innovations/bio-innovations/6485-revision-des-lois-de-bioethique-en-2018-pas-sans-les-citoyens?print=1&download=0&id=6485 Visited on 11 Nov. 2017.
150. CCNE opinion 126 of 15 Jun. 2017 on societal demands for medical assistance in procreation.

B. *Infertile Couples and Parental Project*

259. MAP is a remedy to infertile couples or also to prevent the transmission to the child or to a member of the couple of a particularly serious disease. The pathological nature of infertility must be medically diagnosed (Article L 2141-2 CSP). The man and woman in the couple must be living, in childbearing age and consent prior to embryo transfer or insemination.

If the couple separates, the MAP or embryo transfer are not possible. Situations covered are: the death of a member of the couple, the filing of a petition for divorce or legal separation or termination of the community of life, and the revocation of consent in writing by man or the woman given to the doctor in charge of implementing MAP.

C. *The In Vitro Fertilization and Embryo Transfer*

260. An embryo cannot be conceived in vitro only in the context of MAP with the gametes of at least one member of the couple (Article L 2141-3 CSP). The couple can consent in writing to attempt a fertilization of several eggs for parental project. It may also agree in writing that the embryos, that cannot be transferred or retained, being subject to a research.[151] Both members of the couple whose embryos are stored are consulted annually in writing about whether they maintain their parental project (Article L 2141-4).

A human embryo cannot be designed or used for commercial or industrial purposes (Article L 2141-8 CSP).

D. *The Fate of Embryos*

261. If they have no parental project or in case of death of one of them, both members of a couple or the surviving member may agree their embryos to be received by another couple[152] or to be subject to a research,[153] or that the cells derived from them enter a preparation of cell therapy for exclusively therapeutic purposes,[154] or finally to end the conservation of their embryos.

262. The consent is given in writing and must be confirmed in writing after a reflection period of three months. In case of death of one member of the couple, the survivor may be consulted before the expiration of one year from the date of death, unless any earlier initiative from the couple.

If one member of the couple who was repeatedly consulted does not answer, storage of embryos is ended after five years. The same process is applicable in case of disagreement between the couple on the parental project or on the fate of the embryos.

---

151. Under the conditions set by Art. L 2151-5 CSP.
152. Under the conditions set by Art. L 2141-5 and L 2141-6 CSP.
153. Under the conditions set by Art. L 2151-5 CSP. Modified by Ordonnance 2016-800 du 16 Juin 3016 'Recherches impliquant la personne humaine'.
154. Under the conditions set by this article and Art. L 1125-1.

E. Terms for Embryo Donation

263. For the donor couple, both members of the couple may agree in writing that the stored embryos are used for the parental project of another couple (Article L 2141-5). When both members of a couple, or a surviving member, have consented to the donation of their embryos and that these embryos cannot be used within five years, the conservation of these embryos is ended (Article L 2141-4 CSP).

In case of death of a member of the couple, the surviving member is consulted in writing on the question whether he agrees that the stored embryos can be donated to another couple.

264. The receipt of embryos by another couple is subject to a decision of the judicial authority, which first receives the written consent of the couple at the origin of its fertilization. The judge must ensure that the applicant meets the conditions to access to the MAP[155] and proceeds to all investigations to assess the hosting conditions that the couple is likely to provide to the unborn child on the family, educational, and psychological level. The authorization of reception is issued for a period of three years and renewable.

The principles of anonymity and no compensation are respected: couples cannot know their respective identities.[156] No payment, regardless of form, may be allocated to couples who have given the embryo.

Implantation of the embryo is subject to rules of sanitary security. Only public or private non-profit institutions which have an authorization for that purpose may store the embryos that are to be implanted and implement the procedure.

F. Artificial Insemination with a Third Donor

265. Artificial insemination with a donor can be implemented when the transmission of a particularly serious disease to the child or a member of a couple is at risk, when the techniques of MAP within the couple cannot be a success or when the couple duly informed denies medical assistance for procreation within the couple (Article L 2141-7 CSP).

Spouses, partners bound by a civil union[157] or domestic partners who, for reproductive purposes, use medical assistance requiring the intervention of a third-party donor must first give, as provided by the Civil Code, consent to judge or notary (Article L 2141-10 CSP).

G. MAP or In Vitro Fertilization Performed Abroad

266. Only embryos created with the gametes of at least one member of a couple and in compliance with the fundamental principles of inalienability and of non-patrimoniality provided for in Article 16 to 16–8 of the Civil Code may enter in or out the field of this Code. These movements of embryos are exclusively designed to allow

155. Provided for in Art. L 2141-2 CSP.

156. Nonetheless, in case of therapeutic necessity, a doctor can access to non-identifying medical information about the couple having renounced to the embryo.

157. Pacte civil de solidarité Art. 515-1 à 515-7-1 du Code Civil.

the continuation of the parental project of this couple; they are subject to the approval of the ABM (Article L 2141-9 CSP).

H. The Import of Donor Gametes

267. The import and export of donor gametes or of germinal tissue of the human body are subject to authorization by the ABM. Only an establishment holder of a licence for the MAP can get permission to import or export gametes or germinal tissue (Article L 2141-11-1 CSP).

The authorization is granted if the gametes and germinal tissues are in compliance with the standards of quality and safety in force.[158] Any violation will result in the suspension or revocation of this authorization by the ABM.

I. The Storage of Gametes

268. Any person whose medical care is likely to impair fertility or whose fertility may be prematurely impaired can benefit from the collection and storage of his gametes or his germinal tissues, to the subsequent implementation, for his benefit, of a medical assistance for procreation or for the preservation and restoration of his fertility. This collection and the storage are subject to the consent of the person concerned and, if appropriate, that of a holder of parental authority or legal guardian, if the person concerned, major or minor is subject to a measure of legal supervision (Article L 2141-11CSP).

III. The Rules of Good Clinical and Biological Practise of Medically Assisted Procreation

269. Good practices of MAP are binding provisions of medical care for patients in all clinical and biological processes of the MAP, whether made within the couple or with the third donor.[159] They complete the laws and regulations in this area. They define rules to ensure the quality of work, safety of gametes, germinal tissues, and embryos as well as the risk management. They provide quality guarantees for personnel, premises, equipment with the introduction of quality assurance systems, procedures, records for traceability, and vigilance. Since 2017 gamete donation is allowed to persons who have no child.

---

158. And with principles provided for in Arts L 1244-3, L 1244-4, L 2141-2, L 2141-3, L 1241-7 and L 2141-11 of the Public Health Code and in Arts 16 à 16-8 of the Civil Code, may be subject to authorization.

159. Last update: Arrêté du 30 Juin 2017 amending the Decree of 11 Apr. 2008 concerning the rules of good clinical practice and biological medically assisted procreation www.agence-biomedecine.fr.

A. Medical Record

270. In order to follow-up a couple involving both biological and clinical procedures, a common medical record clinical and biological is established. If it is in an electronic form, the record should be in compliance with laws and regulations of electronic data protection. The record must be retained in accordance with the regulations in force for administrative document storage for twenty years from the last passage of the person concerned in the MAP centre. Beyond this period, it is important to ensure that the confidentiality of personal information is guaranteed.

B. Information of the Couple or of the Concerned Persons (Common Provisions to all the MAP Activities)

271. A fair, clear, and appropriate information on all stages of the care process is given to people involved in these interviews, allowing them to participate in the decision-making process. A multidisciplinary team ensures that the information has been understood, that people were able to ask the questions they wanted and that they got answers to those questions. When necessary, a translator is called.

Each technique is presented with its chances of success and failure, the hardship and constraints, including those which are material/concerning the hardware, or which are financial or psychological, it may cause. Both the side effects and potential risks in the short and long-term are exposed, that are also related to the ovarian stimulation, the surgical and biological techniques that were used. Information is also provided on the existence of the MAP process vigilance.

The information is given to the couple on the likelihood of success in terms of birth, the risk of occurrence of multiple pregnancies and their complications and the state of knowledge about the health of children born after Assisted Reproductive Technologies. Then, the interruption of the process may be immediately considered.

The information also includes the legal obligation of the ABM to assess the possible consequences of the AMPon the health of people who use it and children who were born from these techniques.

The practitioner informs the members of the couple that they may be invited to participate in epidemiological studies, particularly in the above framework, and reminds them theirs rights in the matter.

The couple is informed of the likelihood of conceiving naturally, if necessary after tubal surgery or male urinary tract surgery. Information on adoption is also issued. A complete dossier guide is provided to complete such information.

272. The request is confirmed in writing by both members of the couple, after a minimum period of one month from the last interview. A diagnosis assessment balance is achieved before any MAP. The medical criteria for support are appreciated by the multidisciplinary clinical-biological team.

For each couple and each attempt, the risk-benefit balance in the use of MAP is assessed by the multidisciplinary team. It takes into account in particular the age of the couple, the duration of infertility, the results of the diagnostic assessment, and the risks and efficiency of techniques.

Following this assessment, patients are informed of the test results, diagnosis of infertility and of the proposed therapeutic strategy. The feasibility of the MAP and the time of its implementation are discussed within the multidisciplinary team with the couple, depending on the age of the woman and the man, regardless of the cause of infertility.

273. The multidisciplinary team may at any time vary or refuse care within the limits set by the law and the professional Code of Medical Ethics, insofar as any physician shall consider the advantages and disadvantages of the various investigations and possible therapeutic, and since the laws governing the MAP provide an additional time for reflection when the team considers it necessary in the interests of the unborn child.

IV. Statistics from the MAP

274. The activity of Medically Assisted Procreation in 2015[160] is 145,255 attempts, involving different types of MAPs (insemination, in vitro fertilization and frozen embryo transfers) and different sources of gametes and embryos.

Children born after MAP: according to INSEE, 78,948 children were born in France in 2015. The same year, 24,839 children were conceived after a MAP, representing about 3.1% of children born in the general population this year. A child of 32 is born from MAP in 2015.

We thus note that 5% of children are born with a donation (1,254 children), 3.9% of children from sperm donation (971 children), 1% from oocyte donation (256 children), and 0.1% of embryo donation (27 children). We can estimate that in 2015, in the general population, about 1 in 637 children have been born, thanks to a donation of gametes or embryos.

On intraconjugal MAP, we note that more than a quarter of children born (6,160 children) was designed by intrauterine insemination, the simplest MPAs, less invasive and less expensive. The intrauterine insemination couples come here to confirm their place in the panel of infertility treatments.

A. Gamete Donation

275. In 3.3% of cases, attempts to involve MAP use gametes from an anonymous donor.

The situation of oocyte donation in France remains a concern. Oocyte donation is not sufficiently developed (540 in 2015). Infertile couples who are facing long delays in France are required to travel abroad, where cares do not necessarily meet the requirements of quality and fairness that prevail in France.

In 2015, 29 active centres, 889 in vitro fertilization attempts have been made to the recipient couples. A total of 379 transfers of frozen embryos from donated oocytes were added to in vitro fertilization attempts that year. A total of 1,072 embryo transfers were performed in 2015. A total of 256 children were conceived in 2015 by a donation of oocytes.

---

160. http://www.agence-biomedecine.fr.

In 2015, 540 donors were collected for donation, (2.6%) gave a portion of their oocytes during in vitro fertilization that was performed for themselves. This number is grossly inadequate because, at two couples eligible recipients of oocytes from a donor, 900 additional donors would have been required in 2015 to bridge the waiting list applicants and couples ensure new applications.

276. For the donation of sperm, if the situation is less alarming, however, requires vigilance. In 2015, 255 donations has been accepted The ratio between the number of donors recruited and the number of couples seeking new applications, remains the same: ten per donor recruited .

In 2015, an average of forty-seven specks was made by donor and made available to centres for couple recipients. In 2015, 2,382 couples had an attempt of AMP with sperm donation.

§3. Health Care for Prisoners

I. The Organization of Health Care for Prisoners

A. The Legal and Regulatory Framework in Prisons

277. Since the Act of 18 January 1994, care to prisoners is regulated by the Ministry of Health. Health care is organized under the authority of a hospital medical practitioner with diagnostic missions of diagnosis and care.

Structures for somatic and psychiatric care have been put in place: units (UCSA) of outpatient consultations and ambulatory care and Regional Medical Psychological Services (SMPR).

278. The UCSA is defined by Article D 368 of the Code of Penal Proceedings and organized in conjunction with a healthcare facility nearby. The 189 UCSA spread over the territory provide the physical care: consultations of general medicine, nursing, drug delivery and some specialized consultations and dental care. Laboratory tests can be performed on site. A permanence of care is organized in the absence of caregivers.

The national organization for the hospitalization of detainees is based on the creation of UHSI (secure inter-hospital units) to improve hospital conditions of detainees and rationalize their supervision.

279. Psychiatric disorders are treated in sectors of psychiatry in prison (Service regional medical and psychological) that are attached to a health facility and under the authority of a psychiatrist, a hospital practitioner, assisted by a multidisciplinary team (Article D 372 CCP).

The SMPR (Article R 3221-6 Public Health Code) is responsible for routine care of detainees of the establishment and for implementation of more intensive care for inmates of other penal institutions in the regional sector. The SMPR also provides the psychiatric post-criminal follow-up, in coordination with the sector teams in general psychiatry and child psychiatry.

Under other conditions, for non-urgent and long course care, the Ministry of Justice grants admission to a penitentiary care unit of national range (Article D 393

CPP). Care distribution in those particular health units is specified by Article L 6141-5 and R 6147 of the Code of Public Health.

B. Access to Care

280. The Public Health Code organizes the distribution of care in prisons in Articles L.6112-1 and R.6112-14 and following.

When the health status of a prisoner requires hospitalization in emergency and for a short time, he is admitted in a public hospital or a private institution under specific agreement.

In the other conditions for non-urgent care in the long-term, the Minister of Justice allows the admission to a care facility with a national healthcare establishment for prisoners (Article D 393 CPP). The distribution of care in these health facilities is in accordance with specific Articles L 6141-5 and R 6147-1 and following of the CSP.

C. Specific Measures

281. Pregnancy: if a detainee is pregnant, appropriate monitoring of pregnant women is performed by a healthcare facility in a position to meet his medical condition (Article D 400 CPP). The delivery will take place at this property. If the birth occurs in the place of detention, the birth certificate will mention only the street name and house number. Children are allowed to stay with their mother until the age of 18 months. (Article D 401 CPP).

282. Communicable diseases: specific measures are planned for the prevention of communicable diseases such as tuberculosis (Article D 384-1) and prophylaxis of venereal diseases is organized (Article D 384-2 CPP).

Measures for the diagnosis of HIV infection are taken only with the consent of the individual (Article D 384-3 CCP).

283. Dependencies: dependencies on a licit or an illicit product are supported as well, in collaboration with specialized centres. There are significant differences depending on the institution from abrupt withdrawal with or without psychotropic treatment to substitution with methadone or Subutex.

284. Severe mental disorders: hospitalization for mental disorders is organized by sections L 3214-1 and following of the CSP that provides specially designed units for prisoners. The type of hospital is comparable to that of other mentally ill. The procedures for involuntary hospitalization are set out in Article L 3214-5 of the CSP.

1. The End of Life and the Suspension of Sentence for Medical Reasons

285. Article 10 of the Act of 4 March 2002 provided for the medical release of prisoners ending their life. This provision is part of the Code of Criminal Procedure, Article 720-1-1: 'The suspended sentence may be ordered for a period … that does not have to be determined, for detainees suffering from life-threatening disease or when their health is permanently inconsistent with the continuation of detention …' The circular of 24 July 2004 implements the measure which applies without any regard to the nature and length of the sentence. The decision belongs to the judicial authority for prisoners with definitive sentence, but cannot be applied to defendants who are eligible for release requested by the judge.

To exercise this right, the prisoner must provide a medical certificate to the judge of the application of penalties who will deliver the measure of suspension.

II. The Doctor-Patient Relationship in Prison

286. Article 7 of the Code of Medical Ethics asks the physician to treat with the same consciousness all persons regardless of their reputation or the feelings he or she may have towards the patient … and to assist in all circumstances.

And more generally, Article 10 recalls the duty to respect the rights of persons deprived of liberty:

> a doctor called to examine a person deprived of liberty or to give health care, must not, directly or indirectly, whether by its mere presence, promote or support an attack on physical or mental integrity or to dignity …

> The fundamental principle of free choice of practitioner is not possible in prison. 'Prisoners cannot be examined or treated by a doctor of their choice, unless a decision of the Regional Director of Correctional Services of the territorial jurisdiction'.

Informed consent and refusal of care: in prison, the principle of consent to treatment is respected, the Article D 362 Code of Criminal Procedure states that the prisoner must express its consent under the requirements of the Article 36 of the Code of Medical Ethics.

Concerning the refusal of care and the hunger strike, the will of the prisoner must be respected after being informed of the consequences. No force feeding is possible, unless a risk to life is at stake. Article D 364 of the CPC 'If a prisoner is engaged in a prolonged hunger strike, he or she cannot be treated without the consent, except when the health status deteriorates seriously and only under medical supervision and decision.'

287. Confidentiality and professional secrecy: Article L 1110-4 CSP on respect for privacy and confidentiality of information is applicable to any healthcare professional. Medical examinations in civilian institutions should be performed out of sight of the police. Now the escort for care outside the detention facility is provided by the prison administration, with a police guard during the hospitalization. In some circumstances, because of the dangerousness the prisoner guards are present, and even if they are bound by professional secrecy, that presence remains a breach of confidentiality.

The medical record was previously archived together with the penal record in prison. The medical record is now archived independently from the penal record, under the care and confidentiality of the penitentiary medical service.

The issue of certificates or medical documents: they are delivered to the prisoner upon his request, as provided for in Section D 382 of the CPP, or subject to its express agreement, delivered to his family or his counsel.

§4. Medical Research

288. In 1988, the French Parliament passed a law on the protection of people who are involved in biomedical research so-called Huriet-Sérusclat Act[161] which has been amended several times, in particular by the Act of 2004-806. The law established a legal framework and organized safeguards to protect people participating in the research.

The 'biomedical research is organized and performed on human beings for the development of biological and medical knowledge' (Article L 1121-1, paragraph 1 of the Code of Public Health).

289. Article L1121-2 of the Code of Public Health provides three cumulative conditions: biomedical research is based on the latest state of scientific knowledge and on an adequate preclinical testing. The foreseeable risk incurred is out of proportion to the expected benefit to these people or the interest of this research; finally, research extends the scientific knowledge of the human being and means that will improve his condition.

In addition, biomedical research must be designed to minimize pain, discomfort, fear and any other foreseeable disadvantages related to a disease or research, especially taking into account the maturity for minors and the capacity to understand for adults unable to express their will.

The interest of people who are involved in biomedical research always prevails over the interests of science and society. (These two provisions were added by the 2004 Act).

290. In 2012 a new law has been voted by the Parliament that entered in force in November 2016.[162] The law defines 3 categories of 'research involving the human person' according to the risks: (1) interventional research that involves an intervention on the person not justified by its usual treatment. They include drug trials in accordance with the European Regulation of 16 April 2014 on clinical trials and other research using health products or not; (2) minimal risks interventional research, excluding research on drugs, which involves only minimal constraints, (3) non-interventional research that does not involve any risk or constraint and in which all acts and products are used in the usual treatment.

161. Act 88_1138 of 20 Dec. 1988 as modified.

162. After the publication of the Decree 2016-1537 of 16 Nov. 2016.

I. The Legal and Regulatory Framework for Research Involving the Human Person

291. The research is conducted by an 'investigator' who directs and supervises the conduct of the research; he is a doctor (sometimes he works in collaboration with competent people),[163] with the appropriate skills and experience.

In the research protocol, the medical doctor is not providing care but performing the research.[164] He acts on behalf of a promoter who is a physical person or an entity (laboratory, institute, any research organization) taking the initiative of the research and ensures its management and finance. The sponsor shall provide for free drugs and experimental devices for the research.[165]

A. Prerequisites for Research

292. The promoter must submit a research project to a CPP to get an opinion (on the terms and conditions of validity of the research with regard to the relevance of the research, the risk-benefit balance, the procedures for informing and obtaining consent). The approval of the CPP is necessary to begin the research, as well as the authorization given by the French Agency for the Safety of Medicine and Health Products (ANSM).[166] The promoter must purchase an insurance covering his own liability and any stakeholders', regardless of the nature of his links with stakeholders.

B. Organization of Research Places and Technical Installation for Research

293. Research requires appropriate places. Research sites that are not in care facilities must receive an authorization for a limited period of time. They can be quality controlled by people authorized[167] by the promoter with access to personal data strictly necessary for control. When research focuses on drugs, they are made in compliance with the rules of good clinical practice set by the ANSM.

C. Increased Protection for Certain Categories of Vulnerable People

294. Pregnant women, new mothers, breastfeeding women (Article L 1121-5), persons deprived of their liberty, hospitalized psychiatric patients, persons admitted to a health or social facility (Article 1121-6 of the Public Health Code public), minors

163. Exceptions may be made taking into account the particularities of research in science of human behaviour, odotonlogy, and maieutic.
164. As provided for in Art. R 4127-15 of the Code of Public Health, 'the doctor involved in biomedical research as an investigator must ensure that the conduct of the study does not alter the relationship of trust with his patient nor the continuity of care'.
165. When the research is made in a French public hospital, the sponsor must reimburse the benefits paid or provided by social security as part of the research.
166. The new agency replacing the Agence française de sécurité sanitaire des produits de santé (AFSSAPS).
167. These individuals are bound by professional secrecy.

(Article L 1121-7 of the Code of Public Health), the adults being subject of a measure of legal protection (guardianship and curatorship)[168] or unable to consent (Article L 1128-8 of the Code of Public Health),[169] may be allowed to participate in biomedical research only under the following conditions: either the expected profit is to justify the incurred foreseeable risk, or – research is warranted in view of the expected benefit to other women in the same situation or to their children or other persons within the same legal or administrative status or other minor and provided that research of comparable effectiveness cannot be carried out on another group of population. In this case, the predictable risks and burdens of research should be minimal.[170]

The persons involved in the research must be affiliated to a social security system and have undergone a medical examination. They can never be paid but may receive compensation (reimbursement of the incurred expenses, Article L 1121-11 of the Code of Public Health). There is a national database listing the people who have no affection and voluntarily lend themselves to such research and sick people when the object of the search is unrelated to their medical condition. (Article L 1121-16 CSP).

II. Relationship with the Subject That Lends Itself to Research

295. The physician investigator defines the conditions of recruitment of persons and the criteria for inclusion are assessed by the CPP, as well as the exclusion criteria that can challenge any person for whom participation in the research would be detrimental.

A. *The Information and Consent (Articles 1122-1 and 1122-1-2 Code of Public Health)*

1. The Information

296. People of legal age (18) or emancipated receive from the investigator an information allowing them to give a free and informed consent. The content of information varies with the kind of research.

For interventional research, the information is given orally and presented in a written document that states: (1) the purpose, methodology, and duration of the research; (2) expected benefits, constraints and foreseeable risks, including when the research is stopped before its term; (3) possible medical alternatives; (4) the terms of medical care that are at the end of research, if such support is necessary, in case of a premature termination of the research, and in case of an exclusion of the research; and (5) the opinion of the protection of persons committee (CPP) and the authorization of the ANSM. The investigator shall also inform the subject of the research of his right to receive, during or after the research any relevant information about his health; (6) if

168. Persons under protection measure ' sauvegarde de justice' cannot be solicited for participation in biomedical research.
169. These vulnerable adults may be requested for biomedical research only if research of comparable effectiveness cannot be carried out on another segment of the population.
170. For minors, research are of a comparable efficiency shall not be done on majors.

necessary, the prohibition of participating simultaneously in another research or the exclusion period provided for under the protocol and its inclusion in the national register. The investigator informs the person of his right to refuse to participate in research or to withdraw his consent at any time without any consequences in terms of personal liability.

Exceptionally, where in the interest of a sick person the diagnosis of his illness has not been revealed to him, the investigator may keep secret some information with the agreement of the research ethics committee.

For non-interventional research, performed on request of the medicine agency, the information is limited to the objective, the methodology, and the duration. The information form must be provided to the CPP in the dossier of the research.

At the end of every kind of research, the person may be informed of its overall results. The means of information is defined in the information sheet.

2. The Consent (Article L1122-1-1 CSP)

The 2012-300 law makes a distinction for the consent according to the kind of research.

297. For interventional research the free and informed consent is given in writing or, if not possible, certified by a third party. In an emergency, consent cannot be obtained (Article L 1222-1-2 of the Code of Public Health). In this case, the only consent of the members of the family or of the person of trust[171] is asked if they are present. As soon as possible after recovery, the subject is notified that he or she has been involved in a research protocol. He or she must give his/her consent for following the research, or ask for withdrawal.

For minimal risks interventional research, the informed consent may be oral or in writing.

For non-interventional research the consent is presumed. This means that the subject is informed of the research and of his or her right of opposition. Without an expressed refusal, the non-interventional research is performed.

Regarding secondary use of data, the promoter may ask the subject, at the time of consent, to agree to have his or her data used for further research for scientific purposes only.The person may withdraw his or her consent to such further use or exercise his power of opposition at any time. (Article L1122-1-2)[172]

B. The Information and Consent of Incapable Subjects

298. Non-emancipated minors receive information adapted to their ability to understand. Minors are consulted if their condition allows to seek their personal commitment.[173] Their refusal or revocation cannot be refused. Permission to participate in research is given by the holders of the exercise of parental authority, i.e., by both parents. However, if any of the missing parent cannot give his permission within the

---

171. The person of trust 'personne de confiance' has been set up by the Art. L 1111-6 of the Public Health Code is appointed in writing by any adult who wants to express his or her will so that the person of trust can express them when the person becomes unable to consent.

172. Ordonnance n ° 2016-800 of 16 Jun. 2016 – Art. 2.

173. Articles 1122-2 and following of the code of public health.

time required for the methodological requirements, authorization may be given by the parent who is present if this research presents only negligible risks and constraints and has no influence on the medical care of the minor and when the research is performed during medical care.

Protected adults (guardianship) or incapable of expressing their consent and not subject to a measure of legal protection receive an information adapted to their ability to understand. They are consulted if their condition allows it to seek their personal commitment. Their refusal or revocation can never be ignored.

When the person is under tutorship, authorization shall be given by her guardian and if the CPP believes that the research involves a serious risk of breach to the privacy or integrity of the human body, by the family council (if it has been established), or the guardianship judge. When the person is under curatorship, consent is given by the person assisted and by his guardian. If the CPP considers research involves a serious risk of breach to the privacy or integrity of the human body, the judge supervising a guardianship will be referred to ensure the adult's ability to consent. In case of incapacity, the judge decides whether to allow or not biomedical research.

When adults unable to express their will are not subject to a measure of legal protection, permission is given by the person of trust or family, or by any person closely associated with the person concerned. However, if the CPP considers that the research involves a serious risk of breach to the privacy or integrity of the human body, authorization is given by the judge supervising the guardianship.

§5. Palliative Care and End of Life Care

299. The legislator has organized successively palliative care and end-of-life care. The need for legislation is linked to the fact that doctors have an obligation to deliver the necessary care, and to pursue care even if the patient objects. Medical practice has evolved and many professionals have followed the wishes of patients to set up palliative care. In 1999, the law on palliative care[174] allowed the patient to choose palliative care and set the framework for their implementation.

Despite these provisions, the end of life of some patients remained problematic, and health professionals are still opposed to withdraw from care at the request of patients or their families, because the interruption of care was perceived as the will to cause death. The Act of 22 April 2005 on patients 'rights and end of life'[175] has clarified the conditions under which it is now possible to withdraw from treatment. The law does not really clarify the issue of euthanasia as the text applies to restricted situations.

174. LOI no 99-477 du 9 juin 1999 visant à garantir le droit à l'accès aux soins palliatifs JORF n° 132 du 10 juin 1999.

175. LOI n° 2005-370 du 22 avril 2005 relative aux droits des malades et à la fin de vie JORF n° 95 du 23 avril 2005.

I. Palliative Care

300. The Act of 9 June 1999 recognizes access to palliative care as a right of the patient (Article L1110-9 CSP). The Article L 1110-10 defines palliative care as '*the active and continuing care performed by an interdisciplinary team in an institution or at home. They are designed to relieve pain, calm mental suffering, to safeguard the dignity of the patient and to support his entourage'.* In addition, the patient may object to any investigation or therapy'. (Article 1111-4CSP).

301. A policy is defined for the implementation of the device in the health organization scheme in care facilities[176] through palliative care units, or through alternative structures to the hospital by creating mobile teams for hospitalization at home. Trained volunteers to support the end of life, provide assistance to care teams with the patient's consent for patient comfort and support of the family and relatives. Associations that organize the intervention of volunteers endow a charter that sets out the principles that they must follow in their work. These principles include, in particular, respect for the philosophical and religious opinions of the accompanied person, respect for dignity and privacy, discretion, confidentiality, non-interference in care. When the volunteers involved in healthcare facilities, a Convention organized their activity.[177]

302. The act then provides provisions for the entourage of the patient by creating an accompanying dying person leave[178] amending the Labour Code. Any employee whose ascendant, descendant or a person sharing his home is the subject of palliative care has the right to have an accompanying dying person leave for a maximum period of three months, the leave is not paid. It ends at the expiry of this period, in the three days after the death of the person accompanied.

II. End of Life

303. Despite the introduction of palliative care, end of life is a difficult time for patients and the entourage. Some people, including patients and their families or health professionals want to continue therapeutic care despite their uselessness. One criticisms that patients are subject to unreasonable obstinacy in care, because it is not possible to interrupt the treatment.

304. The law on patients' rights and end of life[179] is to limit unreasonable obstinacy in care. Article L 1110-5-1 of the CSP says:

> The care should not be pursued by an unreasonable obstinacy. They appear useless, disproportionate or having no other effect than artificial life support, they may be suspended or may not be undertaken. In this case, the doctor saves the dignity of dying and ensures the quality of life by providing palliative care.

176. Article L.1112-4 CSP.
177. Art 1O de la loi 99-477 du 9 Juin 1999.
178. Article L.3142-6 to 15 du code du travail (Labour Code).
179. LOI n° 2005-370 du 22 avril 2005 relative aux droits des malades et à la fin de vie JORF n° 95 du 23 avril 2005.

305. To avoid legitimate fear of the patients have their lives shortened, Article L 1110-5-3 of the Public Health Code provides:

> If the doctor finds that he cannot relieve the suffering of a person with advanced or terminal phase of a serious and incurable disease, whatever the cause, in applying a treatment that can have the side effect of shortening his life, he must inform the patient, the trusted person,[180] family or, failing that, a close relative. The proceedings are recorded in the medical file.

The opinion of the person of trust, except in an emergency or impossibility prevails over any other non-medical opinion, with the exception of advance directives in decisions investigation, intervention or treatment taken by the doctor.[181]

Thanks to this law, the patient in advanced or terminal phase of a serious and an incurable disease can decide alone about care. He or she may limit or stop all treatment; the doctor respects the will after informing of the consequences of his choice. The patient's decision is registered in the record.

306. Any adult who is not terminally ill may express his will by advance directives.[182] These advance directives indicate the person's wishes regarding end of life on the terms of limiting or stopping treatment. They may be dismissed at any time. Provided that they have been established less than three years before the unconsciousness of the person, the doctor takes into account for any decision investigation, intervention or treatment concerning the person.

A. *New Rights for the Sick and People at the End of Their Life*

1. Deep Sedation

307. At the request of the patient to avoid any suffering and not to undergo unreasonable obstinacy, the law establishes in the Article L. 1110-5-2 a deep and continuous sedation maintained until death, associated with analgesia and cessation of all life-sustaining treatments.[183] Deep sedation is implemented: 1) in the case of a serious and incurable condition endangering life in the short-term, when the person presents a suffering refractory to treatment; 2) when the decision of the patient with a serious and incurable condition to stop treatment is life-threatening in the short-term and can lead to unbearable suffering.

308. When the patient cannot express his or her will and in the case where the doctor stops a maintenance treatment, a deep and continuous sedation is set up causing an alteration of consciousness maintained until death, associated with analgesia. The deep and continuous sedation is implemented according to the collegial procedure. Deep and continuous sedation can be implemented at home or in a health facility.

180. Referred in the Art. L 1111-6 CSP.
181. Article L 1111-12 CSP.
182. Article L 1111-11 CSP.
183. Law No. 2016-87 of 2 Feb 2016.

2. Advanced Directives (Modification of the Article L.1111-11 by the 2016 Law)

309. Since 2016, the advance directives are binding on the physician for any investigation, intervention or treatment decision, except in the case of a vital emergency (for the time necessary for a complete assessment of the situation) and where the advance directives appear to be manifestly inappropriate or not in accordance with the medical situation.

310. The doctor can refuse the application of advanced directives, when he or she considers that the advanced directives are manifestly inappropriate or not in accordance with the medical situation of the patient. This decision of refusal[184] is taken after a collegial procedure defined and is recorded in the medical file. The refusal is brought to the attention of the person of trust[185] designated by the patient or, failing that, of the family or relatives.[186]

184. Article L 1111-13 CSP.
185. prévue à l'Art. L. 1111-6 CSP.
186. Ar L. 1111-4 CSP.

Part III. The Physician and the Healthcare System

Chapter 1. Relationship with Other Healthcare Providers

311. The relationship between doctors and other health professionals are described in Title III of the Code of Medical Ethics. Code of Public Health defines the framework of exercise of other health professionals and the professional rules of paramedics. The pharmaceutical monopoly and the pharmacy profession are highly regulated in the Book II of the Code of Public Health.

§1. The Ethical Obligations

312. The duties of brotherhood require the physician to respect the free choice of the patient who wants to turn to another doctor.[187] Misappropriation of clients is prohibited.[188] Ethics provides the conditions for the replacement by a colleague,[189] the joint consultation,[190] the treatment in emergency of a patient followed by another professional.[191]

Regarding other health professionals, in the interest of patients, physicians must maintain good relations among them; they must respect the independence of health professionals and the free choice of the patient.[192]

§2. Relations with Other Medical Professions

313. Professions such as dentists and midwives are medical professions who have professional order and are competent in diagnosis and limited treatment; midwives[193] undertake surveillance of pregnancy and childbirth eutocic uncomplicated. Dental

187. Article 60 of the Code of Medical Ethics R 4127-60 CSP.
188. Article 57 of the Code of Medical Ethics R 4127-57 CSP.
189. Articles 65 and 66 of the Code of Medical Ethics R 4127-65 and -66 CSP.
190. Article 64 Code of Medical Ethics R 4127-64 CSP.
191. Article 59 Code of Medical Ethics R 4127-59 CSP.
192. Article 68 of the Code of Medical Ethics R 4127-68 CSP.
193. Conditions of exercise Art. L 4151-1 and following CSP.

surgeons[194] are responsible for diseases of the mouth and teeth. For any act or prescription outside the competence of these professionals, the doctor should be consulted. The professional competence of these is protected by the offence of unlawful practice for any person acting without a diploma. (*See* special chapter on illegal practice).

§3. Relations with Pharmacists

314. The practise of pharmacy is organized around the drug because the pharmaceutical monopoly requires at all stages of the drug chain, pharmacists to be present. According to Article L 4211-1 of the CSP, are reserved to pharmacists, the preparing, the dispensing and the sale of medicines and products for humans and animals, the sale of medicinal plants, essential oils, dietetic foods, and medical devices.

315. The definition of medicinal product by L 5111-1 of the Code of Health identifies the limits of pharmaceutical monopoly. Any product considered as a drug must be dispensed by the pharmacist. There is ample jurisprudence for the delivery of products. If another professional delivers a drug, it is liable to the penalties of illegal practise of pharmacy.[195]

316. The doctor has no right to provide medication to a patient, even for free. Medications are issued on qualitative and quantitative prescription. The doctor is responsible for the prescription while the pharmacist is responsible for issuing. It must ensure that the prescribed dosage is compatible with the health of the patient; there are no drug interactions with other products administered to the patient. In case of doubt, the pharmacist must contact the doctor.

Pharmaco-vigilance however, is the responsibility of the physician who must report to the health authority any complication related to the use of a drug.

§4. Relations with Health Professionals

317. The paramedical professions perform their actions on the qualitative and quantitative prescription doctor. But nurses can perform some actions on their own without prescription or control.

Some health professionals such as nurses, physiotherapists, speech therapists, psychomotor therapists, dieticians, opticians can exercise a professional activity in private practice under individual liability. Others may exercise only as employees of public or private facility care, on medical prescription and under the supervision or the control of a doctor, such as manipulator of radiology and nursing assistants.

The rules of practise of each profession define a list of authorized acts, that the professional can perform alone and those which must be carried out under the direct supervision of a medical doctor.

194. Conditions of exercise Art. L 4141-1 and following CSP.
195. Article L 4233-1csp.

I. Nurses

318. Nurses have a professional order[196,197] and professional rules which distinguish between the acts performed according to their own personal practice[198] and the acts on medical prescription.[199] The list of acts is limited; the nurse is not authorized to perform acts which are not on the list, even under the control of a medical doctor.

There are acts that are allowed with the presence and control of the physician, acts allowed under the condition, provided that a doctor can intervene at any time. And finally, in case of emergency, the nurse can perform acts without medical prescription but with a written protocol dated and signed by the head of department. There are specialties in nursing degrees: nurse specialized in anaesthesiology, operating room nurses, paediatric nurses who have wider competence in their practice.

II. Physiotherapists

319. As nurses, exercise is regulated.[200] There is a professional order,[201] and the professional rules have similar limitations for certain acts. The profession is protected by a diploma, and the offence of illegal practice is sanctioned by Article L 4323-4 CSP.

196. Rules of exercise Art. L 4311-1 CSP.
197. L 4312-1 CSP and following.
198. Article R 4311-3 CSP and following.
199. Article R 4311-7 CSP.
200. Article 4321-14 du CSP.
201. Article L 4321-14 CSP.

Chapter 2. Relationship with Healthcare Provisions

320. Missions of public and private healthcare provisions are described in the Code of Public Health in the Article L6111-1:

> They provide the diagnosis, monitoring and treatment of sick, injured and of pregnant women. They deliver care with accommodation, as outpatient and home care ... They participate in the coordination of care in relation to members of health professions working in general practice and medical and social services, in a framework defined by the Regional Health Agency in conjunction with 'Conseils généraux'. They participate in the implementation of public health policy and organization for vigilance to ensure safety.

321. In France, public and private institutions meet the health needs of the population.[202] The mission of public service includes continuity of care, support of palliative care, university and postgraduate education and research and training of midwives and paramedics (Article L 6112-1 CSP).

General principles characterize the public service mission:

- Equality: duty to accommodate and treat all patients without discrimination (race, religion, ethnicity, age ...), regardless of their health and social status.
- Neutrality: the care is provided regardless of the beliefs and opinions of patients.
- Continuity: the public hospital has set up an organization to ensure continuity of care and reception of emergencies.

This public service mission is not only mainly carried out by public hospitals but also private institutions under certain conditions.

The hospital public service includes private non-profit institutions recognized to provide the public hospital service. Since the Act of 21 July 2009 'Hospital Patient Health Territories'[203] they are called private health institutions of collective interest (ESPIC). Centres fighting against cancer have this status; they provide some missions of the hospital public service in the field of oncology.

§1. Public Hospitals

322. Public health facilities or hospitals are legal persons of public law. They provide a public service and are subject to State control. Depending on the tasks entrusted to them, there are:

---

202. Source http://www.sanitaire-social.com/hopitaux-etcliniques/hopitaux_cliniques_responsabilites_droit/m2/24 En 2011, on dénombre un total de 2 784 Hôpitaux et Cliniques en France, proposant 440 427 lits pour 65.1 millions d'habitants, répartis en:983 établissements publics de santé (284 140 lits),754 établissements privés à but non lucratif (62 645 lits) 1 047 établissements privés (93 642 lits).

203. Reforming the hospital organization and related to patients, health and territories.

I. Regional Hospitals

323. They have a regional focus to provide acute care in medicine, surgery and obstetrics, as well as aftercare and long-term care for the population of the region. They also provide routine care to the nearby population. Some of them are hospital and university centres (CHU), highly specialized care centres, organized in collaboration with the medical faculties for medical doctors, dentists, and pharmacists. They participate in the medical and pharmaceutical research, and in paramedic education.

II. Other Hospitals and General Hospitals

324. They offer services for diagnosis and provide full range of acute care medicine, surgery and obstetrics, as well as aftercare and long-term. Some are specialized in adult psychiatry and in sectored child psychiatry.

Local hospitals (HL) meet the local needs and include only medical activities, aftercare, rehabilitation, and long-term care and provide home and care mainly for the elderly.

Specialized psychiatric hospitals provide care for patients in mental health; the Military Teaching Hospitals (HIA) are placed under the authority of the Chief of Defence Staff, and considered as hospital and university centres by the Hospital Ministry of Health. They also provide care to the civilian population.

Unions inter-hospital include several institutions that combine to exercise common functions, such as in logistics or the use of heavy equipment.

III. Organization of Public Hospitals

325. Hospitals are public institutions enjoying a great legal and financial autonomy. The hospital is headed by the *Director*[204] who is the legal representative of the public health facility assisted by a board called 'directoire' composed of the seven members, or nine in the case of hospital and university centres. The Management Board is chaired by the Director; the Chairman of the Medical Commission Establishment (CME) is Vice President of the Management Board. The other members are the Chairman of the Committee on Nursing and selected members of the management staff of the institution with a majority of medical professionals.

The Supervisory Board 'Conseil de surveillance (CS)'[205] controls the activity of the establishment and validates some decisions. The Supervisory Board consists of nine members in most local hospitals, fifteen in hospital and university centres and all others. It consists of equal numbers of representatives of local authorities, staff representatives, and qualified persons including representatives of users. The Chair of the 'conseil de surveillance' is assigned to a person elected by it, chosen among local elected or qualified persons.

---

204. Article L-6143-7 CSP et D 6143-33 CSP.
205. Article L 6143-5 CSP.

The Medical Commission of Establishment[206] (CME) is the representative body of the medical and pharmaceutical staff of the institution. She is involved with major projects of the institution and plays a role of evaluation. Member of the 'Directoire', the Chairman elected of the Medical Commission Establishment has special skills.

The Commission on Nursing, rehabilitation and medical care[207] is a technical body to advise on the organization of nursing care and support for patients, as well as the training of nurses and rehabilitation. It is also consulted on the institutional plan.

The Technical Committee of establishment[208] is responsible for representing the non-medical staff. It is consulted on policy issues and those concerning staff (working conditions, social policy ...).

§2. Private Hospitals

326. One generally distinguishes among private medical institutions who pursue a profit – which is generally called clinics – and those without profit, which involved most often the public hospital service.

I. General Provisions to All Private Facilities

327. All practitioners who work in a private hospital are members of the medical conference[209] which oversees the professional independence and gives its opinion on the policy of the institution. The annual activity forecasts are communicated to the Regional Health Agency. Employees are represented in the Board of Directors or the Supervisory Board according to the legal nature of the institution.[210]

The medical doctor practising in a private institution must provide the County Council of Physicians the contract that binds him to the institution. The Council checks whether the conditions for the professional independence of the practitioner are met. There should not be any clauses relating to profitability.[211]

II. The For-Profit Institutions

328. Private clinics and hospitals are most often made in the form of incorporated companies or partnerships, in which practitioners perform their private professional activity. In financial terms, the establishment pass through effect contracts with physicians that can be associated or not.

Specialized clinics in surgery provide about 60% of surgery acts performed in France. Centres for Care and Rehabilitation, otherwise known as 'Centres de Soins

206. Article L 6144-1 CSP and following and R 6144-1 and following.
207. Article L 6146-9 CSP and R 6146-10 CSP.
208. Article L 6344-3 and following and R 6144-40 and following.
209. Article L 6161-2 CSP.
210. Article L 6161-1 CSP Ordonnance n° 2010-177 du 23 février 2010.
211. Article R 4127-92 CSP.

de Suite et de Réadaptation' CSSR, involved in the physiotherapy of a patient after a hospital stay for an acute medical or surgical condition. Due to the aging of the population, half of the patients received therein are elderly. Psychiatric Clinics occupy an important place in the management of this type of disease as they make up 30% of all psychiatric hospitalizations.

III. The Non-profit Private Health Facilities

329. These facilities are managed by a legal entity of private law – an association, a foundation, a congregation or mutual – and are not constrained in their internal organization. They are not subject to public procurement rules (but are nevertheless invited to be inspired), their bookkeeping follows the rules of private law, and the profits generated are reinvested in innovation and development of new services for the benefit of patients.

However, their funding is the same as that of public hospitals, and they share the same values and principles: equal access to quality care for all, day-night hospitalization, possibly in emergency, continuity of care during hospitalization, and if necessary orientation to structures taking into account the precariousness of the patient's social situation. They provide patients with preventive, curative or palliative most appropriate care.

330. Private institutions of collective interest 'établissements privés d'intérêt collectif (EPIC)'[212] were able to develop synergies and cross-disciplinary skills to offer comprehensive healthcare support. This is particularly the case of structures medicine, surgery and obstetrics and follow-up and rehabilitation care. This logic also runs structures home healthcare services such as nursing home care – and the facilities housing dependent elderly people 'Etablissements Hébergeant des Personnes âgées Dépendantes (EHPAD)'.

They apply the rates set out in Articles L 162-20 and L 162-26 of the Code of Social Security. They propose an offer of homecare and may, in this case employ, private nurses who are paid by the healthcare facility.

IV. Cancer Centres

331. Cancer centres are university hospitals, private non-profit participating in the public hospital service.[213] These are legal entities of private law; they can receive donations and bequests.

Status confers a threefold mission of patient care, teaching, and research focused exclusively on cancer. However, other public institutions also provide the reception and treatment of the majority of patients concerned.

Each centre is administered by a Board of Directors[214] which is chaired by a representative of the State. The Director General of the Centre and the Director of the

212. Article L 6165-5 CSP.
213. Article L 6162-1 CSP and following and R 6162-1 CSP.
214. Article L 6162-7 CSP.

Regional Health Agency attend the board with an advisory vote. The Board of Directors determines the general policy of the institution and deliberates on the facility project.[215]

215. Article L 6162-9 CSP.

Chapter 3. Liability of Healthcare Provisions

§1. Liability of Public Hospitals

332. Repair of an injury sustained in a public establishment is not the responsibility of individual service officer, but of the public institution under general principles of administrative law.

Administrative courts (Administrative Court, Administrative Court of Appeal and State Council) are competent to recognize the liability of the public establishments and to evaluate the compensation that will be paid by the State.

The harmful consequences of a medical procedure or treatment performed in a public hospital are appreciated by the administrative judge, because medical practice in public hospitals is organized in a particular context: the patient is a user of the public service and the hospital practitioner is an agent of the public service, placed in a regulatory status, to accomplish the missions of the public hospital service. But contrary to the public services depending of the State, public hospitals are responsible for damage compensation and have to subscribe to liability insurance. The Act 2002-303 of 4 March 2002 made mandatory the purchase of insurance for all care facilities.

Derogation is possible for institutions that have sufficient financial resources to enable them to indemnify the damage under the conditions equivalent to those resulting from a contract of insurance.

333. Like any citizen, the physician of a public institution is personally liable for criminal offences committed in the exercise of its functions. The fact that the administrative courts repair the damage does not prevent the complainant, to pursue the author in criminal courts, and the prior criminal proceedings does not affect the decision for compensation by the administrative courts.

I. General Conditions of the Responsibility of the State

334. The fault of the service consists of any breach of the public service obligations; it may be the result of one or more agents, the result of a voluntary or involuntary actions, omission or negligence. By characterizing the maladministration, the judge considers the administrative tort impersonal, without attempting to isolate the author.

The fault of the public service is qualified by the judge according to the severity of the dysfunction of the service. The judge evaluates the gap between the allegations and functioning normally expected of the public service, according to the means at his disposal and to the regulatory duties. Within the general framework of the responsibility of the State, there are two types of faults: simple fault and serious fault.

The liability of the State administration is qualified by the judge for simple fault when the service does not present risks, which means that any significant deviation, any organization that does not meet the regulatory criteria will be qualified of simple fault.

However, for the risky activities, the administrative judge will not compensate the damages as easily; the malfunction of the public service should be large enough to be qualified as 'serious misconduct such as to engage the responsibility of the state administration'.

335. Standards of the judge to qualify the fault: The administrative judge assessed according to four standards: (1) the circumstances of time and place, or circumstances of the case and in particular the notion of emergency; (2) the reality of difficulties encountered in performing the public service, taking into account the practical means at its disposal to execute the missions; (3) the predictability of the accident or the occurrence of complications; (4) the behaviour of the victim in respect of the public service when the damage occurred.

336. To recognize the liability of public healthcare institutions, the administrative judge will qualify the fault of the public service, the damage, and the causal link between the fault and the damage. Compensation for damages in administrative courts requires similar conditions to those of civil proceedings regarding the evaluation of damages and the causal link. Similarly, loss of chances is recognized as a damage in administrative liability rules. Except for information, the burden of proof is on the applicant, such as in civil judicial courts.

The fault of the public hospital is a dysfunction associated with medical acts or care organization. The simple fault will be enough to recognize the liability of the hospital if the failure is a wrong organization or a malfunction of the distribution of care, as well as for damage resulting from acts of care usually provided by paramedics.

II. The Liability of Public Hospitals Based on Fault

337. To recognize the liability for hospitals, the administrative judge will qualify the fault of the service. It is therefore necessary to distinguish between medical act and act of care. The administrative judge does not seek to identify who is the professional and who performed the contested act; the author is not implicated; only the nature of the act itself must be taken into consideration.

For acts of care, the administrative judge may refer to the classification of professional acts as defined in the Code of Public Health, according to their technical difficulties. For nursing acts, some are part of the personal role of the nurse who practises them alone, on his or her own initiative (Article R 4311 R-4A 4311-6), others are made on medical prescription with quality and quantity (Article R 4311-7) and some are allowed in the presence of a physician that can intervene at any time (Article R 4311-9). The list of acts is limited for each profession, and those that are not specifically enumerated for a profession, enter the medical practice.

338. Concerning the medical treatments that could cause higher risks, following the rules of administrative liability the administrative judge recognizes the liability of the public hospital only on the basis of a serious fault or a serious negligence. The decision Rouzet[216] states:

216. 26 Juin 1956 Lebon p. 506.

> The liability of the hospital authority is likely to be initiated on the basis of serious negligence in respect of injury caused by the medical acts. Acts that can be performed by a physician or surgeon or acts who can be performed by a paramedic under the responsibility and supervision of a physician in circumstances that allow it to control their execution and to intervene at any time.

For over forty years, decisions rejecting the liability of public hospitals were frequent, almost one in two, when the judge was not able to describe the serious fault or negligence in the medical activity. As a result, the administrative courts were seen as low determined to recognize the liability of the hospital for damages resulting medical acts.

339. On 10 April 1992,[217] the 'Conseil d'Etat' abandoned the 'serious negligence' as the basis of liability for medical acts to retain only the basis of 'faute médicale' (medical malpractice).

In this case, during a Caesarean section performed under epidural anaesthesia, several falls in blood pressure had happened and afterwards a cardiac arrest occurred. The patient still suffers from significant neurological disorders resulting from cerebral anoxia. While the anaesthesiologist was convicted criminally for unintentional injuries, recognizing a criminal offence, the experts appointed by the administrative judge had found that the sequence of events did not isolate an act or a decision that could be considered as malpractice. This is a chain of a series of imprudence, lack of foresight and medical errors. The breach of the rules of art can be summarized 'after the choice of analgesic method with recognized hypotensive effects, the risk of circulatory accident was increased by the administration of two consecutive hypotensive products and the perfusion of plasma at a temperature much lower than that of the body'. It was very difficult to characterize it as a serious negligence. The 'Conseil d'Etat' has just opted for the qualification of a 'faute médicale' or medical malpractice as follows: 'Whereas the errors that were committed and as described in the expert report, the cause of the accident at Madame V, is a "faute medicale" engaging the liability of the hospital.'

This reflects the desire to compensate the complainant despite the difficulties of bringing the evidence of a fault, without challenging the principle of liability found on the fault.

A. *Faults Related to Medical Act*

1. Qualification for the Fault Related to Medical Acts

340. The administrative judge is competent to qualify the fault of the service, but in the technical field of the medical art, the judge will need medical experts to explain the circumstances in which the medical acts have been performed. The medical expert will tell the judge the differences between the behaviour expected from a practitioner normally diligent and conscientious, and the behaviour blamed in the case. The expert will examine whether the medical acts were performed according to the rules of art. The rules of art are not defined by the law or the jurisprudence. They cannot be standardized; they are 'informal, changing, evolving, pluralistic, rules of art are the opposite of standardization'. They are evaluated in each case by experts

217. Arret V . Conseil d'Etat n° 79027 published in Recueil Lebon www.legifrance.gouv.fr.

with reference to scientific publications, the conferences of consensus, and the recommendations of scientific societies where they exist.

If experts agree that the act is clearly a malpractice or a wrong technique and results from the failure by the surgeon of the essential rules of the operative technique, or the forgetting of foreign material in the body after elective surgery, the medical malpractice could be established.

Often the judge will follow the experts' conclusions when the rules of art have been met and medical malpractice will not be qualified. But the judge is not bound by the expert opinions; it may request a new expertise and appreciate the misconduct of public service on other criteria, such as the organization of the service.

2. A Fault Independent of the Public Service

341. While the fault of service is impersonal, in certain circumstances, administrative courts may qualify the personal fault that reveals the man with his weaknesses and rashness and whose behaviour is not justified by the execution of the public service.

The Administrative courts isolate the personal misconduct of the agent by separating from the functioning of service. When the administrative judge considers that there is no connection to the service, the wrongdoer will be responsible for compensating personally. Then it is either a fault of a specific severity with malevolent intention (abuse exercised by a police officer to satisfy a vengeance,[218] a misconduct inexcusable and unacceptable exceeding the average of the deficiencies that might be expected).

The High Court[219]refused to recognize a link with the service for inexcusable behaviour of the surgeon on duty who refused to examine a child and ordered to the intern to perform appendectomy during which the child died.

Similarly, the 'Conseil d'Etat'[220]qualified as misconduct without link to the public service the surgeon's refusal to come to hospital for a gunshot wound when he was on duty at home.

342. Because of the severity of the charges, some cases are submitted first to repressive courts. The repressive courts may sometimes qualify the inexcusable misconduct, but only the administrative courts can decide whether the link with the public service is preserved or not. This is why even some facts that justified serious criminal sanctions will not be qualified as fault with no link to the public service and compensated by the administrative judge. The criteria of the misconduct in administrative liability are autonomous from the criteria of criminal law. There is no necessary coincidence in Case Thepaz[221] the Tribunal of Conflicts held that the crimes of homicide or injury through negligence were not necessarily their own personal faults.

218. CE 28 Juillet 1951 Cocoz GP 2 p.314.
219. CE 18 Décembre 1953 Fresnais Leb. p. 568.
220. CE 4 Juillet 1990 Le sou médical . Leb. p. 972.
221. TC 14 Janvier 1935 Thepaz, Lebon p. 224.

B. Faults in the Functioning and the Organization of the Public Service

343. An obligation of means burdens on the public hospital service. All institutions of public and private care are required to deliver care in accordance with the mission that is recognized by the Code of Public Health in Articles L 6111-1 CSP and L-6111 L 2. In addition, Article 6112-2 specifies additional requirements for public hospital departments that are the obligation of welcoming patients day and night, of providing the equal access of all the care that the condition of patients requires, of organizing to the exit of the patient by ensuring conditions of existence necessary for continuing treatment.

The establishment is required to have adequate means to provide necessary treatment to the needs of patients received depending on the type of establishment. Any breach could be described as misconduct by the judge who will look at it on a case-by-case basis, if appropriate treatments have been implemented and if there was no lack of surveillance.

1. Lack of Informed Consent

344. In public hospitals, the patient must be informed and consent obtained, for the care and diagnostic procedures especially for each intervention of some seriousness with risks. The information is limited 'to the risks normally predictable frequent or severe'. (Article L 1111-1 CSP). The information also covers treatment suites and evolution of the disease.

As in front of the civil courts, the burden of evidence of the information rests with the establishment since it has the duty to inform.

By failing to inform the patient of the aesthetic risks of a surgery,[222] partly predictable, the practitioners have disregarded their obligations and misconduct of nature to engage the liability of the establishment. A tubal sterilization has been performed during a caesarean when it was not established that another pregnancy would have endangered the life of the mother[223] . As it was an intervention on a major aspect of the physical integrity, the public hospital had a duty to obtain the consent of the patient whose mental state was not such that she cannot be prevented in advance of the risks she will be exposed to, in the event of another pregnancyIn another case a pregnant woman wanted to have natural delivery despite the fact that she had caesarian for her first baby. She has not been informed of the risks of womb rupture and the CE qualified the lack of information, in that particular case, as a fault. The baby is quadriplegic and the mother has not been able to be prepared to have a disabled child.[224]

2. Other Kinds of Faults

345. The failures of the on duty service are regularly described as fault of service. But the practitioner can to be sued as an individual by a criminal court. The public

222. CE 17 Février 1988 CHR Nancy RDSS 1988 p. 509.
223. CE 29 Janvier 1988 Labidi JCP 1988 p. 146.
224. CE 27 Juin 2016 n° 386185 Revue droit et santé n°74.

hospital is liable of the inability to contact the surgeons, anaesthetists, and obstetricians during their on duty service.

The judge may qualify the fault in the functioning of the service without having to seek a medical malpractice simply because successive anomalies occurred, neglect or delay of care in relation to the multiplicity of actors, or defects in transmission of results of analysis from the laboratory at the origin of delayed care.

The admission of a patient is pronounced by the director of the hospital after consulting the physician who must assess whether the patient's condition justifies the hospitalization and determine which service is best suited to receive the patient. Any refusal of admissions that would prove detrimental to subsequent patient is still penalized for fault of service, and sometimes the agent causing the refusal may be sued personally for criminal non-assistance to persons in danger: such as a director sanctioned by criminal court in Douai,[225] or an assistant punished by a disciplinary sanction.[226]

Failure to comply with regulations: midwives should alert the physician of any anomalies in the actions that are beyond their competence. The doctor's delayed call will be characterized as misconduct in the organization of the service, and regardless of the severity of the consequences of the act performed by the midwife, when it was possible to obtain in time the intervention of a physician. Because of the delay, the child was born in a state of cerebral anoxia and is suffering from cerebral injuries with complete dependence.

a. Acts Performed by Health Professionals Beyond Their Competence

346. On several occasions, the administrative judge retained the responsibility of the institution for a midwife who tries extraction with a suction cup[227] while this act is within the exclusive competence of a physician, or when the anaesthesia is performed by a nurse[228] unless the anaesthesiologist has been called, or when an anaesthesia for a caesarean section was performed by a nurse when there was no anaesthesiologist on duty.

b. Acts Performed by Interns

347. The status of interns states that the intern is a practitioner in training who performs preventive and diagnostic care, under the responsibility of the practitioner to which he belongs. The intern is involved in the on duty service under the supervision of the head of department. The intern can be alone to manage a delicate situation in an emergency. Administrative case law has traditionally tried to find in the circumstances of each case, whether the emergency justified or not the behaviour of the intern and the acts performed.

Acts performed by interns without authorization shall be compensated for lack of functioning of the service: such as a difficult delivery under general anaesthesia,[229]

225. 20 Décembre 1951 Gaz.Pal 1952 , 1,175.
226. CE 25 février 1976 Alcalay, Lebon p. 114.
227. CAA Nantes 29 novembre 1989 GP 1990, 2 somm. p400.
228. CE 19 février 1986 Augert RDSS 1986, p. 445.
229. CE 14 Octobre 1968 Doukakis JCP 1968, 15668.

an internal cardiac catheterization[230] prescribed and directed by the intern or the difficult removal of a cyst of the neck[231] by a student when the emergency situation did not justify the act.

C. The Presumptions

348. The service user must bring the evidence of the fault of the public service. However, in certain circumstances, the applicant is unable to provide some concrete and specific elements to convince the judge. The latter, with a view to facilitate compensation, could presume the fault of service when it appears to him that the functioning of the service has failed while it was not possible to prove a fault. The decision says: 'disorders observed can be regarded as revealing a malfunction of the hospital service'. This is the case when simple care, such as those provided by nurses, leads to nerve injuries.[232]

When the damage is important and unexpected, this reasoning of presumption allows the judge to preserve the principle of liability based on the fault, and the victim is relieved of the obligation evidence because the judge considers the discrepancy between the evidence to provide and the means available to the applicant.

In nosocomial infections, the major case is the Cohen decision:[233] after a radiculography followed by surgery for disc hernia, the patient had a meningeal infection that was complicated by spinal cord injury with paralysis of the lower limbs. The disability rate was an 80% incapacity. It appears from the report of the experts that no negligence in asepsis could be attributed to the practitioner, but the 'Conseil d'état' considered that the fact that such an infection could occur, however, reveals a fault in the organization or functioning of the hospital service. The hospital is responsible to provide sterile equipment and products.

One might have feared that this decision will cause an increase in condemnations for institutions, but it was not the case because, only a major damage should allow the judge to use the presumption. The presumption was used for an infection occurred following treatment of a sprained knee, which led to the amputation or gangrene occurred in the hours following the biopsy, which led to the amputation.[234] Many nosocomial infections can be treated and leave no sequel, so the number of disputes remains small.

The presumption can be reversed if the establishment demonstrates the contrary evidence such as the origin of the infection originates from an external cause, or when it can be shown that the infection could be acquired in non-institutional care.

The Act of 4 March 2002 provides in Article 101 that the provisions apply to hospital-acquired infections resulting from the activities of prevention, diagnosis or treatment made as of 5 September 2001. The law establishes the principle of liability without fault for the establishment and compensation for consequential damages if

230. CE 16 Avril 1980 CHR Nantes Lebon p. 873.
231. CE 27 Juin 1977 RDSS 1977 p. 528.
232. CE 11 Octobre 1963, Pernin, Lebon p985. CE 18 novembre 1966, Poissy, Leb p. 1099.CE, 10 mai 2017, Mme A, n°390082 Revue générale de droit Médical n° 65 Décembre 2017.
233. CE 9 Décembre 1988 , Cohen, Leb. p. 431.
234. CAA Nancy 14 Décembre 1994 n°93NC00711.

the injury causes permanent partial disability of 24%. The establishment may be exonerated itself from this responsibility when it brings the evidence of an external cause (Article L 1142–1 CSP).

III. Liability without Fault for Risk

A. The Choice of Treatment Presenting Risks

1. The Use of a New Treatment Whose Consequences are Not Fully Known

349. Gomez Decision:[235] the patient was treated of kyphosis using the surgery method of Luque at the age of 15. Following the intervention, he is still suffering from paraplegia of the lower limbs. The Administrative Court of Appeal of Lyon found that by using this method, the surgeon has implemented a new surgical technique, whose consequences were not fully known and that creates a special risk for patients. When the use of such therapy is not necessary for vital reasons, the exceptional and unusually severe complications that are the direct result engage, even in the absence of fault, the liability of public hospital.

2. A Treatment Presenting a Known Risk with Exceptional Occurrence

350. The decision Bianchi[236] is an important step in the administrative case law, but of limited application. The plaintiff asked for compensation of damage resulting of a spinal arteriography after which he remained quadriplegic. No medical malpractice could be established and the resulting complications, according to the expert, were linked to an occlusion secondary to the arteriography. The 'Conseil d'Etat' held that 'when a medical procedure necessary for diagnosis or treatment of a patient presents a risk whose existence is known but whose occurrence was exceptional, of which there is no reason to suggest that the patient is particularly exposed to, the liability of the public hospital is recognized if the execution of this act is the direct cause of an injury unrelated to the initial state of the patient, or with the foreseeable development of his condition, and with a character of extreme gravity'.

This is the clear disproportion between the extreme severity of the medical sequel and a current medical investigation, which justifies the decision.

But the scope is limited because it applies only to a known risk, but exceptional (which excludes both the unpredictable risk on the one hand and complications statistically evaluated, on the other), unrelated to the initial state or changes in the patient, and extremely serious.

The decisions that followed in its application are very few, because the conditions are restrictive. According to the study of Frederic Thiriez,[237] decisions based on

235. CAA Lyon 21 Decembre 1990, Gomez ADJA 1991 p. 126.
236. CE 9 Avril 1993 , Bianchi RDP 1994 p. 1099.
237. ' La jurisprudence Bianchi, Symbole ou réalité, DA ,2001,n°1 p. 9.

jurisprudence Bianchi are few decisions of thirty between January 1994 and April 2000, only seven met the criteria to qualify for liability without fault risk.

3. A Medical Act Without Medical Justification

351. The decision of Joseph Imbert d'Arles[238] is an extension of the application of the Bianchi decision. A 6-year-old child died after a prolonged coma resulting from a cardiac arrest during general anaesthesia for circumcision at the request of the mother. In this case, the medical act was not necessary for diagnosis or treatment of the patient, but was motivated by the religious convictions of parents without any medical justification since the child was healthy and the surgery was not intended to address a physical assault. The 'Conseil d'état' has adopted liability without fault for an act to risk not medically justified.

B. Failure of Health Products and Devices: A New Extension of Liability Without Fault

352. Blood centres, regardless of their legal status public or private are responsible without fault for damages resulting from the use of blood products that they have issued. In the same direction, for a patient infected with the HIV virus in 1985 and died in 1992, the wife received compensation under the Compensation Act of 31 December 1991, for pain and suffering and funeral expenses. The social security has requested compensation for medical care expenses. The liability without fault of the institution was used.[239] The applicant must provide evidence of the origin of blood contamination.[240] To escape liability, the defendant must provide the contrary evidence of the safety of the products provided. If the link with the transfusion is not provided by the transfusion investigation due to the inability to find documents, the judge acknowledged some degree of plausibility in the arguments of the applicant and said that the causal link must be regarded as established, and the institution is held liable.[241]

The responsibility for the use of equipment or devices was classically accepted on the basis of the fault of service, the Conseil d'Etat' changed its case law: the failure of a respirator that has caused the death of a patient shall, without prejudice to any warranty claims against the manufacturer of this device, engage the liability of the hospital, even in the absence of fault on his part.

§2. The Liability of Private Care Facilities

353. In healthcare facilities, various professionals practice their art: medical doctors and paramedics deliver care and other professionals involved in the reception and hosting of patients.

238. CE 3 novembre 1997, Gaz.Pal 1998 1 .1.
239. CAA Nancy 12 Novembre 1998.
240. Law On patient rights 4 Mar. 2002 Art. 102.
241. CE 7 Juillet 2006 GP Recueil, nov.dec.p. 4097.

The care facilities must compensate for damage caused by the fault of the employees as required by Article 1384 of the Civil Code. Employee misconduct will be quasi-delict. The majority of private institutions reward their health professionals, while medical doctors have a private status and are sued on an individual basis.

When a physician is an employee of an institution, according to the care contract, the care facility must compensate the damages linked with the faults committed by its employees.[242] For acts performed by paramedic employees under the direction of a liberal practitioner, there is no relationship of master and servant with the physician as the responsible is the director of the institution. So the direction of the care facility compensates the wrongful acts delivered when they can be identified as such.

For other situations, the damage sustained by a hospitalized patient in a private institution will be compensated by the courts according to the general principles of civil law, which will look into the links between the patient and the healthcare facility, or the fault outstanding obligations. As for the liability of the doctor, the contractual basis of liability care prevails, though no decision of principle defines the obligations of the institution.

The case law is constructed from obligations in the organization of care, supervision, provision of trained personnel, and appropriate equipment to care. Special conditions were chosen to recognize the responsibility in providing blood products.

Some standards are defined by the code of public health for the equipment of delivery facilities, rooms for awakening anaesthesia, and psychiatric facilities. Failure to comply with these standards may be called endangerment of others (*see* Part 1, Chapter 4, §3), or constitute a circumstance aggravating certain violations of physical integrity.

The courts consider there is a contract of hospitalization and care in these words: 'under a hospitalization and care contract binding him to his patient, a private health institution is required to give skilled care with providing physicians able to deliver care in time and limits imposed by their condition'.[243]

I. Contractual Obligations in General Terms

354. As a result of the contract, there is a dual obligation of accommodation and care.

A. The Accommodation Contract

355. The accommodation contract is to ensure the reception of the patient in suitable and safe premises. It is an obligation of result, and the clinic cannot be exempted except by the evidence of an external cause, such as a fire.[244] A safety requirement of results was established for the fall of a patient in the stay in recovery room.[245]

242. Cass 1re civ 26 mai 1999 JCP G 1999 II n° 10112.
243. Cass 1re civ, 15 Déc 1999 Juris-Data n° 004439.
244. CA Aix en Provence, 20 Dec 1962: Gaz Pal 1963, 1,339.
245. CA Versailles 21 Juin 1997: RD Sanit et social 1999 p. 563, obs G Memeteau.

Property of residents must be protected when they are stored by an authorized person of the institution. Article L 1113-1 of the CSP establishes the principle of strict liability in case of theft, loss or damage of objects stored. However, the amount of compensation is limited (two times the maximum amount social security), which implies deposited items should not be of significant value. The hosted person cannot impose the deposit of any object; the use of the deposited object must be justified during the stay in the facility (Article L 1113-4 CSP).

But the limitation is not applicable to persons admitted in emergency or cannot express their will. In this case, if the loss or damage results from an evidenced fault of the institution or its agents, limiting damages is no longer applied.

For not registered or not removed objects, responsibility will be retained in case of proven negligence.

B. *The Contract of Care*

356. In providing care, an obligation of means burden on the institution. Case law has retained various obligations:

– a duty of care and diligence, the patient must prove that a fault has occurred in the usual care or paramedic acts such as injections or post-operative surveillance. General obligation to monitor depends of the patient; it should be strengthened and adapted to the needs and health condition. For example, the responsibility has been held for the fall of a patient under the influence of epidural anaesthesia,[246] or for inadequate supervision of a head injury.[247]

The suicide of a patient does not necessarily mean that the surveillance was not adequate, if suicidal tendencies were not known in the case of defenestration in a cardiology department,[248] the liability for the establishment shall not be engaged. In contrast, the court found that the clinic could not ignore the fact that the patient was exposed to a risk of suicide or accidental fall in the case of an agitated patient, after surgery, who had torn his infusions, runaway in the hallways and had received sedative treatment before he defenestrates.[249]

However, the specialized institutions that receive mentally ill patients with suicidal risk will hold a specialized reception with local security and enhanced surveillance.

Regarding the organization of care, on the basis of Article 1147 of the Civil Code, the liability will be linked to the breach of an obligation inherent in the organization: management, organization, selection of staff, availability of equipment, and medical devices or products.

357. The availability of qualified personnel is a contractual obligation,[250] when a clinic let perform by care auxiliaries acts which are in the field of competence of

246. CA Paris, 16 décembre 1994 Juris-Data n° 024429.
247. Cass Cic 3 Oct. 1967, Bull civ I n° 273.
248. Cass 1 civ, 3 mars 1998, Bul civ 1 n° 90.
249. Cass 1iere Civ 28 avril 2011 n° 10-15289.
250. CA Paris 23 janv 1981: Gaz Pal. 1981, 2, somm p. 206.

nurses, its liability shall be recognized. The clinic that allows a surgeon to practise cosmetic surgery without having sufficient qualification or expertise breaches its obligations to the patient for the implementation of breast implants.[251]

On the organization of the presence of on duty physicians, the clinic committed a fault contributing to the occurrence of the damage by the total vacancy of the continuity of care for more than an hour and a half. The lack of qualified personnel resulted from insufficiently of precise rules in the organization procedure, because doctors are contractually bound to the clinic to ensure continuity of care.[252]

As for equipment, the clinic must provide a material in good condition,[253] fulfilling the required criteria to ensure sterility, and in accordance with appropriate administrative permissions.[254] The equipment must be regularly maintained to ensure proper utilization and checked before each use.

The obligation regarding equipment is an obligation of means, which requires the victim to provide evidence of a hardware failure. If the equipment is well maintained and in good condition, the liability for the clinic will not be considered.[255] However, the self-employed surgeon of the private establishment must verify before use the good functioning of the material at his disposal, and if he does not, his personal liability can be recognized.[256]

II. Specific Obligations

A. *In Providing Blood Products*

358. Clinics have a duty of care and diligence in providing of blood products supplied by a blood centre. In the case of HIV infection after a transfusion, the responsibility of the care facility may be held liable only if the establishment had the technical means to control blood products.[257] Then the victim or clinic will claim a fault of the supplier of the blood (blood centre).

The victim must prove the blood source of contamination, which is especially difficult if the transfused blood product was prepared from multiple blood donations. The compensation fund for victims of blood created by the Act of 31 December 1991 compensates only patients infected with HIV since 1985; for prior contamination, a regime presumption applies, namely a period of occurrence compatible and negative

251. Condamnation in solidum du chirurgien et de la Clinique Cass 1iere Civ 11 Juin 2009 n° 08-10642.
252. Condamnation in solidum Cass 1ière Civ 13 Nov. 2008 n° 07-15049.
253. Cass Civ 28 nov 1961, Bull Civ 1; n° 558.
254. CA Aix en Provence 1 mars 1999: Juris-Data 045235 opération de neurochirurgie.
255. http://www.sop.asso.fr/les-services/juridique-professionnel/materiel-defectueux-quelles-responsabilites-12.
256. CA Lyon, 13 fev 1961 D 1961 p. 634.
257. Cass 1ere civ 12 avril 1995, n° 92-11.950.

factors such as the absence of membership to at-risks groups or sex life exposing to contamination.[258] The same method was applied to the Hepatitis C contamination.[259]

The Law of 4 March 2002[260] indemnifies medical accidents, and nosocomial infections states that the applicant must provide evidence of the origin of blood contamination, or that the defendant must prove that transfusion is not the cause of contamination.[261]

B. *In Compensation of Nosocomial Infections*

359. For infections that develop as a result of hospitalization or care performed at the facility, for a long time the courts wanted to make the evidence of a lack of sterility to recognize the liability of the facility. It was certainly difficult to establish for isolated cases. However, finding of several infection cases developed in the same service was sufficient to establish the origin of the contamination in the hospital and to presume a deficiency in the process of sanitizing the operating room.[262]

In 1999, the Supreme Court has issued several decisions on establishing a safety requirement for results making the care facility liable unless it can prove an external fault or force majeure '*contract of hospitalization and care between a patient and a health imposes on the latter, in terms of nosocomial infection, a safety requirement result he can be released only by providing evidence of an external cause*'.[263]

This requirement has also been extended to the medical doctor, who will have to make the evidence of an external cause; otherwise, he will be liable. If evidence of nosocomial infection is made, but could have been acquired in several establishments, it belongs to all those whose responsibility it is sought to establish that he is not at the origin of the infection.[264]

Since the Act of 4 March 2002, nosocomial infections can be compensated by the national solidarity.

C. *In the Supervision of Psychiatric Patients*

360. The monitoring requirement is an obligation of means for care facilities, and the victim has to make the evidence of a fault. It must be adapted to the patient's condition and to earlier reactions known. However, monitoring is more rigorous as the patient is likely to commit suicide, which justifies the supervision of places and objects. The clinic must take all necessary measures to ensure, even against the will of the patient, the patient safety.[265] Responsibility has been retained if dangerous objects were left accessible to the patient and allowed him to perform his act,[266] and similarly,

---

258. TGI Paris 3 juil 1991 n° 9834/90 JCP G 1991, II, n° 21762 note Harichaux.
259. CA Aix en Provence, 19 janv 1995 n° 95/3331.
260. Loi n° 2002-303 du 4 mars 202 JO 5 Mars 2002.
261. Article 102 de la loi du 4 mars 2002.
262. CA Paris, 17 Oct. 1997: juris-Data n° 358_359, somm.p. 9.
263. Cass 1 civ, 29 juin 1999 FD Sanit et soc p. 570 Obs M Harichaux.
264. Cass 1[ière]. civ 17 Juin 2010 n° 09-67011.
265. CA Bordeaux, 13 Janv 1999 Juris-Data n° 040597.
266. CA, Paris 9 Janvier 1962 Gaz Pal 1962,1, Somm p. 75.

a clinic that does not provide overnight supervision of patients and maintains window without railings door located several metres above the ground.[267]

However, judges do not qualify a fault of the clinic when all the security measures are in place, especially when nothing in the patient's condition should suspect that he will suicide.[268] The patient who committed suicide during a medically authorized release does not assume any responsibility for the clinic. The exit permit is given by the doctor who is responsible for its decision and shall provide the necessary measures.[269, 270] For patients who commit damage to third parties on outings authorized test, no-fault responsibility will be recognized.[271]

D. *In Obstetrics*

361. The liability is based on contractual obligations, as for all private institutions. However there are standards in personnel and equipment for obstetric clinics.

Midwives should be able to provide pregnant women the necessary care. The responsibility of the clinic will be retained if a midwife is not able to provide a postpartum needed care, or do not monitor monitoring patient by qualified staff or to take the necessary initiatives in the absence of a physician.[272]

Effective coordination between midwives and obstetricians is essential. Midwives are authorized to make eutocic deliveries and should alert the physician for all other deliveries they are not allowed to do as well as for the use of forceps. They have in this context, the obligation to alert a doctor or obstetrician immediately.[273] If the midwife does not call to the physician on duty, a fault of the facility will be qualified to the clinic.[274]

III. Joint Liability

362. In some circumstances, it will be difficult to separate which part of the damage each professional caused. The doctor and the institution will be sentenced to pay compensation 'in solidum' for the whole damage. And each has a duty vis-à-vis the other, and their respective insurance conclude agreement to pay the common debt.

In surgery, when there is a joint fault in the surveillance by the paramedical staff, and a fault in the organization of post-operative care from the doctor, they were recognized liable 'in solidum'.[275]

In obstetrics, front of the difficulty of separating the respective acts causing the damage, if a midwife does not notify the doctor anomalies on monitoring, which

267. CA Bordeaux 18 Janv 1990 Juris-data n° 040426.
268. Cass 1 civ 9 dec 1968 D 1969, Somm p. 51.
269. Cass 1ier. Civ 10 juin 1997 Juris-datan° 002632.
270. Cass 1ier. Civ 10 juin 1997 Juris-datan° 002632.
271. Cass 1ier. civ, 7 mai 1981 Bull civ 1, n° 118.
272. Cass 1re civ 1 juin 1976 JCP G 1976, II, 18483, note R Savatier.
273. Article L 4151-3 CSP.
274. CA Nancy, 24 nov 1966, JCP G 1967, II, 15066, note Savatier.
275. Cass 1 Civ 24 janv 1995: Juris-Data N° 000760 gangrène gazeuse ayant nécessité une amputation.

delayed the intervention of the doctor and compounded the suffering of child, the court criticized as well the doctor who was not concerned by the situation of the woman whose labour was particularly long.[276] Similarly, the accumulation of successive negligence: neglect of the midwife who has not met the deadline for monitoring postpartum, the nurse who did not check blood pressure and the obstetrician who has not looked for the extension of the tear of the womb neck.[277]

276. CA Montpellier 3 Mars 1999 Juris-data n° 034048.
277. CA Paris 4 juil 1997 Juris-Data n° 022613.

Selected Bibliography

Alt-Maes *La loi sur la fin de vie devant le droit pénal* JCP G 2006 1, n° 119.

Auby J.M. *Droit de la santé* Thémis 1981; *Traité de droit médical et hospitalier* Litec.

Auby JM *Les aspects administratifs de l'Assistance médicale à la procréation et des prélèvements sur le matériel biologique humain* Petites affiches numéro spécial 'Bioéthique' 14 December 1994 n° 149.

Aumonier N, Beigner B. Letellier P. *L'euthanasie* PUF Collection Que sais-je? 2001.

Boyer-Chammard et Monzein P *La responsabilité médicale* Ed 1974.

Byk Christian *La loi relative au respect du corps humain* JCP ed G 1994,1, n° 3788.

Budet JM. *La réforme de la transfusion sanguine* Cahiers hospitaliers, oct 1999, n° 150, p. 21.

Cadoux L. *Informatique et libertés en 1997, vers où allons-nous? Eléments de perspective.* Gaz.Pal, 16–17 avril 1997 p. 2.

Chabas F. *la responsabilité du médecin et du biologiste envers l'enfant en matière de procréation médicalement assistée.* Gaz Pal, 7–8 mai 1999, doctr, p. 16.

Clavel E. *Considérations sur la clause de conscience du médecin après la loi du 31 décembre 1979* JCP 1985, I, n° 3192.

Cohen P *Un point sur l'infraction de mise en danger d'autrui* L'entreprise médicale, 20 Decembre 1999, n° 196.

Cormier C. *La chirurgie esthétique* RDSS 2002, p. 724.

Dictionnaire permanent Bioéthique et biotechnologies Les éditions législatives.

Dierkens R. *Les droits sur le corps et le cadavre de l'homme* Masson 1986.

Dorsner-Dolivet A. *L'indemnisation des dommages médicaux après la loi Kouchner* RGDM 2003, n° 9, p. 60.

Dreifus-Netter F. *La filiation de l'enfant issu des partenaires d'un couple et d'un tiers,* RTD Civ 1996, p1.

Dreifus-Netter F. *Adoption ou assistance médicale à la propcréation: quelles familles?* D.1998, Chron, p. 100.

Dubouis L., *La réparation des risques sanitaires,* RTDSS.2002, n° 4.

Duguet AM Chaluleau C Dubail G Revuelta V *Abus, fautes fraudes. 10 ans de jurisprudence du contentieux du contrôle technique de l'assurance maladie de Midi-Pyrénées.* Journal de médecine légale et droit médical 1999 Vol 42, N° 7–8.

Duguet AM *La faute médicale à l'hôpital* Ed Berger-Levrault, Deuxième édition 2000.

Duguet AM *Jurisprudence professionnelle des certificats médicaux* Ed berger-Levrault 2001.

Duguet AM, Beviere B, Boucly G, Rial E, Cambon-Thomsen A. *Les droits des patients et les Bio sources. L'utilisation des éléments du corps humain.* J Méd Légale Droit Médical, 2007, 50 (1–2) 55–62.

Duguet AM, Esperou H, De Guerra A, Cambon-Thomsen A. *Le cadre réglementaire du don de cellules hématopiétiques: la Directive 2004/23/CE Etat de la transposition en France et en Europe (projet POSEIDON)* In Accès aux transplantations d'organes et de tissus en Europe Droits aux soins en Europe Les Etudes Hospitalières Bordeaux 2009.

Duguet AM *La responsabilité du fait des actes médicaux et de soins dans les établissements publics* Traité de médecine légale et de droit de la santé Vuibert 2010 p. 589–600.

Duguet AM *Responsabilité professionnelle des médecins* Traité de médecine légale et de droit de la santé Vuibert 2010 p. 601–614.

Duguet AM *L'accès aux soins des détenus* in L'accès aux soins: principes et réalités; presses de l'Université de Toulouse 2011 p. 129.

Dupont M, Esper.C, Paire Ch *Cours de droit hospitalier* D.2009, 7 ed.

Durand-Zaleski Isabelle, Chevreuil Karine *The French health Care system*, 2011 in International Profiles of health care systems 2011.

Feuillet B. *Les fondements du secret médical* Responsabilité sept 2001 n° 3 p. 25.

Feuillet B. *Procréation médicalement assistée et anonymat* Ed Bruylant, 2009.

Frayssinet J. Pedrot P. *La loi du 1ier Juillet 1994 relative au traitement des données nominatives.* JCP ed G 1994, II, n° 3810.

Glorion Bernard, Hoerni Bernard *le secret médical. principes généraux* Droit médical et hospitalier Editions du Juris-Classeur 2004.

Gaumont-Prat H. *Le principe de l'anonymat dans l'assistance médicale à la procréation et la révision des lois de bioéthique,* Dr Famille 2001, Chron n° 2.

Gaumont-Prat H. *Droit des produits de santé: actualités de l'année 2008* LPA Juin 2009 n° 113.

Guigue J. *Le secret médical. Principes juridiques fondamentaux* Droit médical et hospitalier Lexis Nexis SA 2005.

Harrichaud M. *La preuve de l'information médicale* RDSS 1998, n° 1, p. 68.

Selected Bibliography

Harichaud Michèle *La responsabilité médicale et les établissements d'hospitalisation privée* Traité de Droit médical et hospitalier Ed Litec 2000.

Harrichaud M. *Les droits à l'information et au consentement des usagers du système de santé après la loi n° 2002–303 du 4 mars 2002* RTDSS 2002, p. 673.

Hoerni B. Benezech M *Le secret médical: confidentialité et discrétion en médecine* Masson Collection Abrégés, 1996.

Huriet C. *La protection des personnes se prêtant aux recherches biomédicales. Le rôle des comités: un bilan et des propositions.* Rapp Sénat n° 267, 2000–2001.

Labbée X. *Condition juridique du corps humain avant la naissance et après la mort* Presses Universitaires de Lille 1990.

Labbée X *L'expérimentation médicale,* Médecine et droit, n° 11, 1995, p. 10.

Laude A *La traçabilité des produits de santé,* Patites affiches, 8 février 2001, n° 28 p. 7.

Lenoir N. Mathieu B. Maus D. *Constitution et éthique biomédicale* Doc Franc 1998.

Malaurie P. *Commentaire de la loi du 22 Avril 2005 relative aux droits des malades et à la fin de vie* Defresnois 2005, p. 1385.

Mathieu *La recherche sur l'embryon au regard des droits fondamentaux constitutionnels* D 1999 Chron 451.

Mémeteau G. Mellenec *Traité de droit médical* Ed Maloine 1982.

Memeteau G. *La responsabilité hospitalière de la clinique privée* RTDSS 1997, p. 96.

Mémeteau G. *Le refus de soins à l'enfant conçu* RD sanit.soc 1979, p. 317.

Mémeteau G. *Avortement et mère incapable: vers l'avortement forcé* RTDSS 1983, p. 525.

Mémeteau G. *Cours de droit médical* Deuxième édition Les Etudes Hospitalières 2003.

Paricard S. *La consécration d'un droit à l'avortement?* Dr Famille 2009 n° 9.

Paricard S. *La recherche médicale et le droit: une relation ambivalente* RDSS 2009, 98.

Penneau J. *Faute civile et faute pénale en matière de responsabilité médicale* Ed 1975.

Penneau J. *Protection de la personne dans le domaine de la recherche biomédicale* RID comp 1998, 383.

Penneau Michel *La protection pénale du cadavre* Journal de médecine légale et droit médical, 1996–1997.

Ponchon F *Le secret professionnel à l'hôpital et l'information du malade* Ed berger-Levrault 1998.

Prieur S. *La répression judiciaire du délit d'entrave à l'IVG* Petites Affiches, 5 novembre 1997, n° 133.

Rougé P. *La transfusion sanguine* PUF, Paris 1997 coll Que sais-je?

Roujou de Boubée G. *L'interruption volontaire de grossesse: commentaire de la loi du 17 Janvier 1975:* D.1975, chron.n° 209.

Rubellin-Devichi J. *Procréations assistées et stratégies en matière de filiation* JCP ed G 1991, I, n° 3505.

Sargos P. *Obligation d'information et risques graves,* Médecine et droit 1998, n° 33, p. 14.

Soutoul J.H. *Le médecin face à l'assistance à personne en danger et à l'urgence.* Ed Maloine, 1991.

Tavernier M. *Les soins palliatifs* PUF Que sais-je? 1991.

Thouvenin D. *La personne et son corps: un sujet humain, pas un individu biologique* Petites Affiches numéro spécial bioéthique, 14 Dec 1994, n° 149.

Thouvenin D. *La responsabilité médicale* Ed médecine Sciences Flammarion 1995.

Traité de droit médical et hospitalier Ed Litec.

Veron M *Responsabilité pénale médicale Atteintes involontaires à la vie et à l'intégrité de la personne* Droit médical et hospitalier Editions du Juris-Classeur 2002.

Veron M. *Responsabilité pénale médicale Autres cas de responsabilité pénale* Droit médical et hospitalier Editions du Juris-Classeur 2002.

Verspieren P. *Face à celui qui meurt (euthanasie, acharnement thérapeutique, accompagnement)* Ed Desclée de Brouwer, 1984.

Vivant M., Le Stanc C., Rapp L. Guibal M. *Droit de l'informatique,* Ed Lamy.

Vulliet-Tavernier S. *Après la loi du 6 août 2004: nouvelle loi informatique et libertés, nouvelle CNIL.* Dr.Soc.2004, n° 12, p. 1055.

Index

The numbers here refer to paragraph numbers

Index

Index

Made in the USA
Monee, IL
13 September 2026

62974262R00096